W0013622

MARKETING TO MUMS

HOW TO TARGET BRITAIN'S MOST POWERFUL CONSUMERS

JESSIE WILSON

Marketing to Mums: How to target Britain's
most powerful consumers
Jessie Wilson

Copyright © 2017 Jessie Wilson. All rights reserved.

ISBN : 978-1981107490

No part of this book may be reproduced in
any manner whatsoever without prior written permission
from the author, except in the case of brief quotations
embodied in critical articles and reviews.
All enquiries and requests relating to this book should
be directed to the author.

Product trade names or trademarks mentioned throughout this
publication remain property of their respective owners.

The material contained within this publication is for information purposes
only. The author and publisher accept no responsibility or liability for any
investment decision made on the basis of this information or for any
inaccuracies, or omissions contained from hereon in.

DEDICATION

*To my mum, Patricia, for running alongside me
and constantly pushing me towards the finishing line,
and to my amazing daughter Timi for introducing me
to motherhood and making it all worthwhile.*

CONTENTS

INTRODUCTION

Q. What makes over 75% of women change how they shop?

A. Motherhood

Mums hold the keys to the kingdom when it comes to household spending, influencing over £250 billion in expenditure every year. This buying power alone qualifies mums as one of the most critical demographic segments for brands. They are the primary decision makers when shopping for family holidays, cars, food, housing, clothing, consumer electronics, products and services for their children, and so much more. And yet few companies invest enough time or money in trying to understand this key segment of the population, often shoehorning them into an impassive, one-size-fits-all category.

All too often, motherhood is represented as a series of

mundane tasks to be completed, or worse, shown through a lens of pastel perfection. This lack of understanding of the true intricacies, complexities and nuances of motherhood prevents brands from connecting with mums on an emotional level, and precludes them from reaching their full potential.

Marketing to Mums encourages you to look beyond the three-letter word that is used to describe the complex and varied group of women with kids, offering tips and tools to help shape and adapt your marketing and business practices to better embrace the mums you are trying to reach. Peppered with case studies and anecdotes from influential industry leaders that have been successful at marketing to mums, the book provides a framework that will enable you to duplicate success in your industry.

The book has been designed in such a way as to lead you through the steps that I typically follow when working with clients in-person to help them come up with a comprehensive marketing plan. We begin with strategy and how to incorporate the voice of the customer into our thinking and our long-term marketing plans. This discussion leads naturally into the topics of targeting and positioning, and more specifically, how to identify which types of mums you should be focusing your marketing energies on, and how to make your offering to them stand out. From here we move on to a discussion of the so-called 4Ps of marketing – product, price, promotion and place – and look at how to translate this strategy into specific actions.

The remaining chapters look at some of the issues that companies face when trying to sell to mums, including branding, social media management, and how to integrate press coverage into your wider marketing efforts. We then look at some examples of companies that are doing a particularly good job of marketing to mums, before finishing with a more detailed look at the way mums shop, and how to maximise their customer experience to ensure brand longevity.

Whether you are a marketing manager, a sales representative, a customer services manager, a small business owner, or simply an individual with an idea for a great product, this book will broaden your understanding of marketing and help you identify the many parts that go into developing a coherent and effective marketing strategy and plan.

Whatever your background, I hope you find this book useful. I have been fortunate in my career to have worked with some amazing brands, many of which are featured in this book. I hope that this book will leave you inspired and feeling optimistic about the future. It is an absolute pleasure to be able to bring you some of the tips I have picked up over the years, and I hope you enjoy reading this book as much as I have enjoyed writing it.

Jessie Wilson

A NOTE TO SMALL BUSINESSES AND SOLOPRENEURS

We were all young once

A few months ago, I met a woman who was looking for help launching her new subscription-box business. When I mentioned established subscription-based businesses, Graze and ToucanBox, she stopped me. "I can't compete with the likes of those," she said. "They are completely different in scope and scale."

Such thinking is not uncommon among entrepreneurs and small business owners, many of whom are daunted by the biggest and most successful companies in their industry. But as I always point out, most companies started out small – even those that are now multinational behemoths.

ToucanBox, for example, was founded in 2012 by Virginie Charlès-Dear, who stumbled upon the idea after looking for ways to entertain her then 4-year-old. "I thought to myself how wonderfully convenient it would be if I could get a tailor-made selection of [craft] materials and activities delivered to my door," she explains on her website. "So, the next day, I went out and made a mock-up. When my daughter eagerly requested a second box as soon as she'd finished the first, I knew I was on to something." Fast-forward five years, and the company now ships over 100,000 boxes to destinations around the world every month, and is reportedly worth in the region of £17 million.

Snack-box provider Graze has similar humble origins. "The company began in one of our spare rooms and has grown very quickly," said Ben Jones, one of seven friends who founded the business in 2008. The company now employs over 500 staff, and has been valued at £300 million, making it the fastest-growing food retailer in the UK.

With over four new online subscription box businesses entering the UK market every month, according to susbscriptionradar.co.uk, competition is tough, and sadly, few manage to attract enough subscribers to ensure their long-term profitability. For some, it is due to their inability to recognise what customers want. For others, failure can be attributed to the wrong execution of their growth and marketing.

Of course, this is not unique to the subscription industry. Many founders struggle to grow their businesses, which is why it is so important to spend some time analysing the strategies of some of the larger players that have successfully targeted mums, and look at what worked for them (and what didn't), and identify whether there is anything in their strategies that we can incorporate into our own business plans. It's easy to dismiss larger, more-established firms as playing in a different league, but I would contend that these are precisely the sort of companies that we should be looking at and drawing inspiration from.

In the pages that follow, you will find numerous examples of large brands that have done a stellar job of marketing to mums. Some will be more relevant to your business than others, but all have been carefully chosen as examples of how to market to mums the right way. I therefore ask that as you progress through this book, you keep an open mind to the lessons that can be learnt from looking at the experience of these larger firms, and remember that they were all once where you are now: questioning the best way to successfully market to mums.

"

Your assumptions are your
windows on the world. Scrub
them off every once in a
while, or the light
won't come in.

"

- Isaac Asimov

1.

THINK YOU KNOW YOUR MARKET?
THINK AGAIN

Mums: You either are one, have one, or know one

We all have an image in our minds of what we believe a mother looks – or at the very least *should* look like. Mention the word *mum* to just about anyone, and the mental image they draw will likely be just as unique as they are. Most will either conjure an image based on interactions with their own mother, or will draw from their own experience of being a mum or living with one.

But as we all know, mums are a diverse group. For every mum who thinks that co-sleeping provides the key to a good night's sleep, there will be another who insists on a set bedtime with everyone sleeping in their own beds. For every mum who follows a strict routine, there will be another who thinks that you should go with the flow. And for every mum that reads the instruction manual when they buy a new appliance, there is a mum who will chuck it in the bin and figure it out herself.

When targeting mums, it is important to set aside your own personal notions of what it is to be a mum. Even if you are a mum yourself, you need to accept that you are but one example. You may consider yourself to be a perfect example of the type of customer you are trying to attract, but ask yourself this: How many other mums are exactly like you? Can you really speak for all the mums in your target market?

You may *think* you have identified a gap in the market and developed a really great product, and perhaps you have. But how can you be certain? Sure, you can ask your family and friends, but can you really rely on them to tell you the truth? And even if you can, are their views really representative of the large pool of mums that you hope to sell to?

You might ask for feedback in private Facebook groups you belong to, or upload a photo of your product to Instagram. This will undoubtedly result in a handful of feel-good responses from people telling you that they would definitely buy it, and might even net you a few sales. But here's the rub. People will try to be nice to you, and avoid confrontation, because they know this idea is your baby, and they don't want to burst your bubble.

Trade fairs such as Kind Und Jugend in Cologne and the Harrogate International Nursery Show are full of products that been designed by parents who believe they have come up with a unique solution to a common parenting problem.[1] Some of these products are truly innovative. Others border on the ridiculous, often just replacing one set of problems with another.

Take the extra-long sleeveless bib that we saw at a baby and toddler show a few years ago, for example. My colleague Anja and I nodded politely as the product's creator explained how she had spent 6 years working on the bib. "It was one of those light bulb moments" she told us. "A bib that is long enough to be placed underneath the child's plate, not just keeping the child's clothes clean, but also the table."

As parents ourselves, Anja and I could instantly see some issues with the design (not least the propensity for broken dishes), and it seemed other parents at the fair agreed, with several picking up on the fact that the bib needed to be ironed in order to make it flat enough to stick to the table. None of the parents we spoke to felt the bib merited its £30 price tag.

To discover that parents aren't interested in your product after you've spent 6 years developing it must be soul-crushing. Imagine investing your life savings into developing a product only to find that nobody wants it. Sadly, though, it's not an uncommon scenario.

According to Bloomberg, 8 out of 10 entrepreneurs who start businesses fail within the first 18 months.[2] And while there are no statistics for companies specifically targeting mums, anecdotal evidence suggests that the survival rate among companies marketing to mums is equally poor.

Every year, the Baby Products Association runs a competition to find the 'next big' baby product.[3] Designers and entrepreneurs are invited to present their products to a panel of judges in a Dragons' Den style format. Yet of the twelve finalists selected by the BPA between 2010 and 2013, only two have managed to avoid joining the nursery scrapheap: Monkey Swimmers foam armbands, and the 5 Point Plus Anti-Escape System – a car seat accessory that prevents toddlers from being able to wriggle out of their seats.[4] Both are clearly fantastic products (the latter recently received the endorsement of industry giant Maxi Cosi).[5] But it is no coincidence that of all the entrants, these are the two brands that invested the most time and money in market research and eliciting feedback from prospective users *prior* to bringing their products to market. All twelve finalists cited their own personal experience as the inspiration behind their products. And on the surface, all seemed great ideas. But ultimately, only two were able to turn their ideas into a profitable business.

According to CB Insights, who painstakingly analysed

more than 200 post-mortem essays written by start-up founders and investors, the single biggest reason why companies fail is lack of market demand.[6] That should be self-evident. If no one wants your product, your company isn't going to succeed. But many start-ups operate under the misguided belief that if they build it, consumers will come.

Too many entrepreneurs rely on assumptions when trying to build their businesses. They assume that if they are struggling with something, others must be too. "I don't like having to clean my child's high chair after every meal, so others mustn't either."

Others mistake demand for *a* solution as demand for *their* solution. They naively assume that because they hear mums complaining about food getting stuck in the crevices of their babies' high chairs, there will be sufficient demand for a bib that can sit underneath their child's dinner plate, when in actual fact, the solution might be as simple as replacing the high chair with one that is easier to clean.

Feedback is your friend

The sooner you accept that all your assumptions about whether mums are going to buy and use your product are simply that – untested assumptions – the better off you will be. The last thing you want to do is spend six years squirrelled away working on a product that nobody wants to buy. Harsh as it may sound, assumption and extrapolation in the absence of quality data will nearly always lead to failure.

Marketing decisions should never be based on what you would do if you were your own customer. You have a biased viewpoint and are emotionally invested in the brand you are promoting. And because of that, what you think of your product or service is irrelevant.

Remember, you are not building your product for yourself. You may be a user of it, but you are not your target market. You can control all the inputs, but you will never be able to see your product or service the way that the consumer sees it.

It's what experts refer to as the humility of marketing: putting aside your own supposedly superior viewpoint and accepting that your customers' perception of your product or service is the only one that matters.[7]

"Have I priced my product too high?"

"Have I got the right balance between functionality and design?"

"How effective is my website at delivering the key benefits of my product or service?"

When faced with questions such as these, your response must always be, "I don't know."

Recognising that you are not the consumer, but that you can connect with them to get the answers you need, is paramount for any effective marketing strategy.

To that end, it is essential that you start collecting feedback from your target market NOW, if you haven't already. Not just from your family, friends and online connections, but from the wider pool of parents that you are trying to reach.

The feedback you receive won't always be positive, but that's not necessarily a bad thing. Negative feedback is like pain in the body: it tells you something's not quite right. Maybe it's telling you a feature isn't needed or that there's a problem with how something works, or that there's a fundamental flaw with your product's design. Or perhaps it's telling you that you are not communicating your product's key benefits effectively.

The criticism you receive from potential customers and the questions they ask about why they should consider trialling your product will, at times, seem foolishly short-sighted. Why can't they see the benefits that are so obvious to you? They must be crazy if they think what you are offering them won't make their lives easier / their children happier / their businesses more successful. But what if the problem lies more with you than with them? Could it be that you simply aren't communicating the value of what you are offering them in the best possible way?

Business owners often look down on people who don't instantly recognise the value of what is being put in front of them. Potential customers who aren't interested in their product are dismissed as fools, and the company keeps plodding along on the same course, pushing the same product in the same way for much too long.

Though negative feedback can be hard to swallow, when dealt with appropriately, it can be far more valuable than receiving a glowing testimonial. Without feedback, you're left to guess how your decisions impact the market and the level of demand for your product or service. Requesting criticism might feel awkward, but when you take the time to listen and respond properly, negative feedback can result in you taking action and making enhancements that propel your business to the next level.

Marketing is as much about listening as promoting

Marketing is about so much more than simply getting your message out to consumers. It is about understanding mums, connecting with them, figuring out which ones in particular you want to target, working out how best to talk to them, and of course, learning from them. It is about doing your homework *before* you rush ahead with an ambitious advertising campaign.

You may have already been told by many that your idea is genius. You may have received backing from investors, and perhaps even picked up some industry awards for innovation. But unless you fully understand the needs and desires of the market, and truly understand the mums you want to sell to, your business will never reach its full potential.

If you want your product to be successful, you have to start connecting with your consumers from the outset. Don't rush into execution and tactics without carving out your strategy. Put as much effort into gaining a steady stream of feedback and traction as you do developing your product, and you can't go wrong.

Stop making excuses

You can probably think of several reasons why you feel you're not able to do consumer research. Budget constraints, lack of time, a fear of the unknown, thinking you know best, Steve Jobs didn't do any market research. Believe me, I've heard them all:

1) **Cost: I simply don't have the money to do research.**

Instead of focusing on the cost of doing research, consider the benefit to your company that the research will bring. Good research will always pay for itself, through improved product design, greater knowledge of your customers and better market understanding. Moreover, as we shall see in Chapter 2, market research needn't be expensive. There are plenty of ways to generate data from your current and prospective customers without breaking the bank.

2) **Time: I need to get my product into the marketplace ASAP. Taking time away from my launch activities to go out and collect feedback would slow me down too much.**

Understanding market needs up front significantly increases your chances of a successful launch. After all, how can you possibly target your product effectively if you don't fully understand who your audience is and how they will likely respond to what you are offering them? Before your design is set in stone, ask probing questions that explore and explain prospective users' behaviours, problems, workarounds, irritations, and obstacles. The data you collect can also be used in your launch materials and press packs to add weight to your campaign.

3) **Fear: I'm worried that if I start telling people about my idea, someone else will steal it and build a business just like mine.**

I hate to break it to you, but the likelihood that someone is going to suddenly drop everything, spend thousands of pounds and lots of late nights developing a product just because they heard you talking about it is very slim. But if you are really worried about this happening, why not get them to sign a non-disclosure agreement?

4) **Arrogance: I've been in the industry a long time and know the market and my customers well. There's nothing market research could teach me that I don't already know.**

When you've been in the market a while, it's easy to make assumptions based on past experience. The problem is, once assumptions are made, they have a habit of quickly turning into fact, and before you know it, you're spending thousands of pounds to fix something that didn't even need fixing in the first place. Don't let your ego prevent you from listening to the mums you hope to serve. Give them a chance to provide their input, and you may be surprised what you learn.

5) **Steve Jobs didn't do any market research, and he didn't do too badly.**

In actual fact, Steve Jobs did do market research – quite a lot of it, in fact.[8] As did Henry Ford (who famously said that if he'd relied on consumers to tell him what they wanted, he'd have put all his efforts into breeding a faster horse).[9] Their great leaps of innovation may not have come from any specific customer-driven insight, but once their ideas were born, research played a critical role in ensuring their products were as good as they could possibly be.

At some point, you just have to "embrace the suck" of marketing, to borrow a phrase from the military. You may feel nervous seeking feedback from strangers, but putting it off isn't going to do you any favours. It's just going to put you behind. Get out there and talk to your target consumers. And, if they tell you that they want a "faster horse," don't stop the conversation there — explore the reasons for that desire. It's a lot cheaper to find out if your product hits the mark while you're still in the development phase than to launch a flawed product and have to play catch-up later.

Over to you

Try to identify at least three key assumptions that you have made about the wants and needs of mums as they relate to your product category or industry, and think about how these assumptions have shaped your marketing decisions to date. Use the questions on page 13 as a guide.

UNDERSTANDING YOUR MARKET: KEY QUESTIONS

- How well do we understand the marketplace? Are we listening and responding to the needs of our customers and keeping track of our competitors' activity?

- What are some of the dissatisfactions felt by mums in our industry or product category? How do these rank in order of importance to mums?

- How do mums make their purchasing decisions? What do they want? What do they need? How do they buy? When do they buy? How involved are their partners and children in the decision-making process?

- How long will our product or service be used for, and how will it be disposed of?

- What are mums' first impressions of our product? Is our packaging pleasing to the eye? How will mums respond to the ingredients and raw materials used?

- What sort of mums are most interested in our product or service? Do we appeal to a diverse group of mums or to a smaller, more concentrated segment of the market?

- Are we effectively communicating why our product or service is better for mums and more responsive to their needs?

"

Research is creating
new knowledge.

"

- Neil Armstrong

2.

MARKET RESEARCH THAT PAYS

Whoever understands mums best, wins

Many people think of market research as a tool used only by big brands. While it is frequently used by large companies to fine-tune their products – from the colours used in their packaging materials to the position of their product on the supermarket shelf – market research can also serve as a powerful catalyst for growth in smaller businesses. This is particularly true when it comes to marketing to mums. With so many companies relying on their own biased assumptions regarding what mums want and need, investing in market research is a sure-fire way to give yourself a winning edge over your competitors.

The value gained through added insight into the market and your customers should not be underestimated. Although research for early-stage companies is often limited by time and budget constraints, if done properly, market research should pay for itself many times over through future sales and a shorter path to success.

The aim of this chapter is to provide you with an understanding of how to use market research and market information to test the validity of your business concept and refine your product or service to make sure it sells.

Step 1: Formulate your questions

Before launching any new product or service, you first need to assess market size, market dynamics, and level of demand for the product or service in question. The key questions you should be asking yourself are:

1) Is the business concept viable?

2) What are the major risks and information holes and what information is needed to address and minimise these risks?

3) Is our strategy and business model likely to succeed?

It is generally not efficient to broadly research a market area without first identifying the key assumptions and unknowns upon which success of your product or service proposition hinges. Therefore, the more questions you find yourself asking, the better.

For example, you might be considering introducing a CV-writing service aimed at mums looking to return to work after an extended childcare break. Before pushing forward with the idea, it is important to make sure that there is sufficient demand and interest in the service to justify you spending time and money building up the business. Some of the issues you might want to address before going public with your service include:

- Is there a real need for this service?

- Is the market large enough to turn it into a standalone business?

- Is what I am offering enough to compel mums to sign up for careers help from an unknown company?

- What sort of timeframe will mums be looking for when using a CV-writing service, and is this feasible?

- Can the service be sold at a price that will enable profitability of the venture?

Alternatively, you might be considering launching a mobile app to help parents connect with others in their local neighbourhood. As before, the first step would be to confirm that there is sufficient demand to justify investing

17

time and money into developing the app. You would then want to research the existing methods mums use to meet fellow mums, and ascertain the number of mums who use existing Tinder-style apps to find friends, and in the process, find out what they like and dislike about such apps.[10] You might also want to investigate whether this is a service mums would consider paying for, and if not, look for ways to monetise the service without compromising user experience. Remember, however excited you are about your idea, turning it into a commercial venture requires input and feedback from the parents that you aim to serve, every step of the way.

Whether you are marketing a product or service, launching a new brand or reigniting an established one, the starting point is always the same. Begin by identifying what questions you need to ask, and what research data you need to gather. Never begin market research without a clear goal in mind. The aim is to derive smart information from the research that relates directly to important questions – questions that shape your marketing programme and allow you to operate more successfully in the future.

Step 2: Desk research

There are two main types of market research that can be used to find out about customers' needs and buying habits. Primary research is data collected directly from the customer, typically through interviews, surveys and focus groups. Secondary, or desk-based research, conversely, is data that already exists or may have been collected for another purpose, and includes reports and studies by government agencies, trade associations or other businesses within your industry.

Since it is typically faster and easier to use data generated by others, secondary research is usually the first step in collecting market information. There are a number of sources for collecting secondary data, including:

- Industry reports compiled by market research firms, stock analysts and industry experts

- Government agencies and census bureaus

- Media reports and trade journals

- Competitor literature and websites

- Industry organisations

When used correctly, secondary data can be hugely beneficial in helping you identify key industry trends, gather much of the aggregate customer and market data needed to develop market size and growth estimates, and perform initial competitor analysis.

The UK Office of National Statistics (ONS) is one of

most plentiful and wide-ranging publically-available sources of information.[11] Although their data tables can be a little tricky to navigate, it is worth spending some time exploring their website. The ONS covers many topics and trades – ranging from sales volume and revenues at homeware stores, for example, to household spending broken down by number of children.[12] Also available are census results, company data, and reports on regional and national business patterns. Additionally, any ONS-compiled statistics not currently available on their website can often be accessed by submitting a Freedom of Information Act request, which in most cases, simply involves sending a short email outlining your requirements.[13]

Another good source of information is the business section of your public, or local college or university, library. The services provided vary from library to library but usually include a wide range of government publications with market statistics, a large collection of directories with information on domestic and foreign businesses, and a wide selection of magazines, newspapers and newsletters. If you are near London, it is also worth registering to use the resources at the British Library, where you can gain electronic access to more than £5m worth of the latest market reports from leading publishers such as Frost & Sullivan, Passport and many more.[14]

Research and trade associations are useful for collecting industry-specific data, and depending on your industry, you might find some of it in the public domain. Other information will only be available to members who have paid a membership fee. However, the research gathered by the larger associations is usually thorough, accurate, and often more than justifies the cost of membership.

Newspapers, journals, magazines, and radio and TV stations provide another valuable source of information. Keep in mind though that not all research quoted in the media is created equal. The data might be a few years old, or it may be biased, or there might be flaws in the methodology. As such, I would caution any reader from placing too much weight on statistics they have seen quoted in the media without checking the underlying source. Rarely are survey write-ups in the media accompanied by information disclosing problems such as low response rate or respondent misunderstanding of specific survey questions.

When reviewing secondary data, you must learn to read between the lines and consider any problems that might have clouded the final results. Try to view your secondary research findings collectively, and use them objectively to identify key trends and developments in your industry, rather than taking the information presented in any one report as gospel.

Step 3: Primary research

Although secondary research is a great place to start, on its own, it's seldom enough. Relying on the published work of others will never give you the full picture within the context of your own unique business, and can leave you blind you to potential obstacles and opportunities that have the power to make or break your business.

Spending a few days collecting secondary research will help ensure you don't waste valuable time gathering data that others have already collected, but it will not put you inside the heads of the mums that you are hoping to target. As such, desk research should only ever be thought of as the starting point for your research, rather than as an alternative to conducting more in-depth primary research.

There is no substitute for getting out and conducting interviews and seeking feedback from the actual group of mums to whom you plan to market your product or service. John le Carré wrote in *Tinker, Tailor, Soldier, Spy*, "a desk is a dangerous place from which to view the world".[15] This is as true for business managers and entrepreneurs as it was for le Carré's spies, and should serve as a reminder of the importance of getting out and talking to mums, rather than making assumptions based on your own prejudiced viewpoint.

While the data you collect from primary research is often messy, contradictory and inconclusive, the insights gained from direct interaction with potential customers can be invaluable. Unlike secondary research that is generally easy to come by, however, acquiring good quality primary research can prove a little more tricky. It can be hard finding mums willing to spend time answering your questions, particularly if you are interested in a specific cohort of mums, such as those who have purchased a cot-bed within the past 12 months, which was a request that one of my clients recently came to me with. In this case, you might want to consider enlisting the help of a specialist market research agency that can help you source respondents.

If you do decide to recruit your own research participants, make sure that you recruit a broad enough sample to ensure your results are meaningful. Keep your questions simple and focused, and be careful not to introduce bias into your questions, or worse, lead your respondents into telling you what they think you want to hear. Nice as it is to be told that your idea is great, it is important to remember that the aim of your research is not to feed your ego, but to elicit honest and objective reactions from your future customer base.

To get the most out of market research, it is important to think about how you are going to use the data you derive from the research, and how it might help drive forward the very idea or concept that spawned the research in the first place. All too often, businesses commission research without having a clear purpose in mind. Think about what you want you want to achieve with your research and formulate the questions with this in mind.

That may sound like you're making assumptions about what the data will reveal long before the research has been executed, but this is not the case. The true skill in market research lies in the ability to visualise the charts and tables in which the research results will be presented, without making any assumptions about the actual data contained within them.

Once you have prioritised your information needs, the next step is to identify which research tools best fit your requirements. There are four main types of research that you might want to consider:

1) **Interviews**

    Interviews with mums and other potential users of your product or service should form part of nearly every market research plan. They are often the best and most efficient way of testing assumptions and gaining an intuitive feel for mums' requirements and needs. Typically ten to twenty interviews per product category will be sufficient to understand most customers' needs. Spend time in advance developing interview guides to make sure you cover key issues, and ask open-ended questions that encourage mums to talk. Finally, be considerate of mums' time. Few will want to spend more than half an hour answering your questions.

2) **Surveys**

Surveys are mostly used to validate customer need and market characteristics. They are not typically used at the concept or planning stage unless you are trying to ascertain specific market statistics that will help determine the viability of your business proposal. The most important aspect of any survey is making sure that you ask the right questions in such a way that it minimises respondent fatigue and early dropout. In order to make sure the results are meaningful, it is also important to understand the statistical representativeness of your sample to ensure that the results can be extrapolated to the wider population. If in doubt, always ask someone proficient in survey design for help. It might cost you more initially, but you will never regret paying for good quality insight.

3) **Focus groups**

A focus group is a small group of invitees who, guided by a trained moderator, discuss a product, a service, their perceptions of a particular company, or specific issues relevant to them. Like interviews, focus groups run the risk of not being representative. Therefore, the focus group should never be your sole source of information, and should instead be used as a form of validation and insight into issues affecting mums and their needs. Focus groups take time to assemble and research participants will usually expect to be compensated for their time. For this reason, they are not generally used at the concept stage, or when budgets are tight.

4) Ethnography and direct observation

Ethnographic research is a technique whereby researchers observe how consumers go about their everyday lives. It stems from the idea that what people say, what people do, and what people say they do are entirely different things.[16] Although more time-consuming than the other three research methods detailed above, it can be the most rewarding. Often, the best insight comes not from inviting consumers to take part in focus groups and surveys, but rather from watching how they interact with various products in their own environment, and identifying any problems they might be facing. Procter & Gamble is a big proponent of this method, training all new R&D personnel in what it calls immersion research. The consumer goods giant has even been known to send senior managers to spend time in low-income homes around the world in order to understand what matters to their customers in terms of their desires, aspirations, and needs. The company claims this has led to many effective innovations – including laundry detergent with more noticeable suds.[17]

Whichever method you choose, try to focus your research on learning about mums' needs, not just their reaction to your specific concept. Market research is a process for listening and learning. Use it properly, and you will be rewarded with a more visceral and empathetic sense of what mums are seeking, which in turn, will enable you to make better and more informed decisions.

Step 4: Map the market

The fourth and final step in the market research process is to build a market segmentation. Effectively just a fancy name for a plan or map of the market, market segmentation refers to the process of defining and breaking down a wide market into clearly identifiable and homogeneous groups with similar characteristics and traits.

For example, if you were to segment the restaurant market in the UK, you might find that it looks a little like Fig. 2-1, with the shaded areas showing gaps in the market.

FIGURE 2-1: Sample segmentation of the UK restaurant market

	Hamburgers & Hotdogs	Fish	French	Italian	Chinese	Indian
Upmarket waiter service		Seafood restaurants	French restaurants	Italian restaurants	Chinese gourmet restaurants	
Medium-priced waiter service	American-style cafes and diners		French bistro-style cafes	Pasta restaurants	Chinese restaurants	Indian restaurants
Fast food & takeaway	McDonald's, KFC etc	Fish & Chip shops		Pizza parlours	Chinese takeaway	Indian takeaway

MARKET GAPS = OPPORTUNITIES

Few organisations are big enough to satisfy the needs of an entire market. Most companies are forced to focus their attention on specific segments and select only those that they are best equipped to handle. The purpose of a market segmentation is to convey the different options available to consumers in a clear and concise way that enables you to strategically identify where to focus your marketing efforts.

Not all market segmentations will highlight such clear opportunities for market entrants to differentiate themselves from the existing competition as the example above – in fact, very few will. However, by building a

28

comprehensive overview of the market in this way, and populating it with figures indicating the market size of each segment and the market share held by the leading players, it should at the very least become apparent which areas of the market are over-saturated, and which offer the most opportunities.

It is important to note at this stage that segmentation and targeting are fundamentally different. Segmentation is about identifying all the different options open to your target consumers, and seeing how your proposition fits in with these. It is an analytical process driven by consumer needs, and if done properly, will help you maximise resources and enable you to develop more effective and better targeted marketing campaigns by comparing the relative merits of your product or service with that of your competitors.

Targeting, on the other hand, is about determining which segments to go after with your marketing efforts, and comes later. Many marketers conflate the two, but in my experience, this is a mistake, since only by understanding the market as a whole can you even begin to carve a niche for yourself. As I often tell my clients, jumping into targeting without first conducting an objective critique of the market is a bit like trying to launch a kite without first assessing the wind conditions. You might manage manage a successful launch first time around, but more often than not, it will end in a flop.

Over to you

Make a list of the areas you need to research and try to identify any gaps in your knowledge and understanding, and start thinking about how to address these. Next, think about all the different options available to mums in your industry, and try to map out the market in a way that's appropriate for your business. It might take time, but if done properly, it will help focus your marketing decisions and lead to better targeting decisions.

COMMON MARKET RESEARCH MISTAKES TO WATCH OUT FOR

- **Poor Sampling**. If you ask the wrong people to answer your questions, your whole analysis can be flawed. Always be sure to define your sample at the start. Write out who you want to talk to and why. Define the rules which will, in turn, define who is included in the audience.

- **Lack of focus**. Think about why you are conducting market research and what you are hoping to achieve *before* starting the research. Frame short bullet points that outline the aims for the project and the type of knowledge and understanding that is required. It's easy to find data that loosely relates to your industry or business, and conducting research without a clear goal in mind can be an exercise in futility.

- **Researcher Bias**. Everyone has their own opinions that influence the way they rationalise data. The trick is to recognise this. By understanding what your bias is, even if it's simply that you want your business to work no matter what, and then you can be wary of it when analysing the data you've gathered, and take an extra step to find an alternate way to make sense of it.

- **Ambiguous Questions**. If your question isn't precise, implies bias or has a vague meaning, then you will struggle to derive meaningful insight from your data. Think about how you will use the information, and ensure there are no gaps or overlaps in available answer options that might confuse respondents.

- **Survey overkill**. Surveys are great, but more often than not, they are too long, too complicated and too engineered. Keep it short by only asking what you need to know.

" "

You never really understand a person until you consider things from their point of view.

" "

- Harper Lee

3.

TRIBES AND TAPESTRIES

Tribe (n): a group of people with similar values or interests

A few months ago, I posed a question to my Institute of Mums community of over 100,000 mums, asking them to suggest "tribes" or classifications that they felt they could identify with. Between them, they came up with over 100 different groups.

Many of the suggestions I received were based on demographic classifications such as mums of toddlers or mums of pre-schoolers, while others focused more on behavioural and psychographic traits, such as mums who shop in Lidl versus mums who shop in Waitrose, as well as my personal favourite, mums of shit sleepers! Others focused on events such as pregnancy and trying to conceive, in many cases breaking these down into smaller segments such as VBAC mums (mums opting for a vaginal birth after previous caesarean) and Rainbow mums (mums who have had a baby after a previous loss). And interestingly, several of the suggestions related not to women's roles as mothers, but rather to their experiences as individuals – for example, mums who keep fit, mums who play instruments, mums who bake, and mums who work in finance.

The point of this exercise was not to pigeon-hole mums into arbitrary categories, but rather to shed some light on the multiple threads that both separate and unite mums, and highlight the fact that there is so much more to being a mum than simply raising kids.

Few mums today fit the so-called "traditional 2.4 children" mould that is so often marketed to them.[18] A third of Britain's working mothers are the main earners in their household,[19] and over a quarter of mums are raising children as single parents.[20] Nearly one in three mums giving birth in the UK in 2015 was born outside of the UK, rising to over two thirds in London.[21] And contrary to what the ad-men might lead you to believe, over half of mums giving birth for the first time in 2016 were unmarried.[22]

Brands that are successful at marketing to mums do not tend to think about mothers as one homogeneous group. They refrain from making sweeping generalisations, and take into consideration the different dynamics of mums. They recognise that their product or service will not be relevant to all mums, and instead focus on the segments or tribes that offer the best fit. This attention to detail helps them build up a complete picture of their ideal consumer, and in turn, enables them to speak to their consumers as individuals, rather than simply seeing them as one monolithic group united by their reproductive status.

That's not to say that there aren't common threads that are relevant to most mums, because there are. We know that most mums today are seeking products and services that save them time, offer value, deliver comfort and pleasure to their families, are healthy and socially responsible. But it's not enough to build a marketing strategy on these facts alone.

When I work with clients, I often encourage them to adopt what I call the tapestry approach to target marketing. The idea is simple. Think of each individual customer as an intricate tapestry, with each thread in the tapestry representing a different identity, experience or preference. The threads from which mums choose to weave their tapestries might be similar, but the final result will always be unique to them.

As marketers and sales people, it is our job to pinpoint which threads are relevant to our brand, and identify the tapestries in which these threads are most prominent. The tapestries comprise our target market, but it is our recognition and understanding of the component threads that will enable us to formulate a marketing strategy that resonates with mums.

One of the best examples of this approach can be seen in a 2017 TV campaign promoting Kraft Macaroni and Cheese (sold in the UK as Cheesey Pasta).[23]

Rather than focus on the product's key benefits (minimal effort, full of flavour, one pot preparation), Kraft instead decided to look at some of the character traits shared by the mums who might buy their boxed easy-to-prepare foods. What they came up with was genius. Kraft hypothesised that the sort of mums who might opt to periodically feed their children macaroni with cheese sauce from a packet were also the mums most likely to swear. They tested this assumption with an independent survey of 1,000 mums, and found that three quarters of mums under the age of 35 have indeed sworn in front of their children. This single statistic formed the basis of their entire campaign.

For the campaign itself, Kraft partnered with Melissa Mohr, author of Holy Sh*t: A Brief History of Swearing, to create a short two minute film, which they released in the lead up to Mother's Day. The film starts with Mohr giving mums cute alternatives to swear words such as, "What the frog?" and "sons of motherless goats". These alternatives are intended to help mums "make things right," with the message that if they don't, "there's always

Kraft."

"Mums make mistakes. Even the best mums," Rachel Drof, marketing director for Kraft Macaroni & Cheese, said in a press release about the campaign.[24] "We wanted to cut mums some slack [and] embrace their imperfections."

With organic, vegan and gluten-free foods making gains at the supermarket, the campaign offered a subtle nod to the guilt some mums feel when feeding their kids a quick meal of pre-packaged macaroni and cheese. At no point do Kraft claim that Mac and Cheese is the perfect dinner to feed your kids. Instead, the message they send to mums is "don't be too hard on yourselves," with the campaign firmly centred around the insight of "perfectly imperfect parenting," as Drof puts it.

The advertisement was an instant hit, attracting over 1.5 million YouTube views in less than 24 hours. Mums around the world praised Kraft on social media for their honest portrayal of motherhood. And then, importantly for the brand, they went out and bought Kraft Mac and Cheese. According to analysts, sales of Kraft Macaroni & Cheese skyrocketed in the month following the campaign.

Smart targeting

In order to fully connect with your target consumers, it is important that you learn how to talk to them as individuals and not simply as mums. If you can identify some particular behaviour or experience relevant to your brand that forms part of how mums define themselves, then you are on track to create a winning marketing strategy.

When I asked my community of mums to suggest names for their mummy tribes, not one person suggested mums who *can't* cook or mums who *don't like* to cook. And herein lies the genius of the Kraft campaign. Rather than try to go after the arbitrary category of mums who don't like cooking – a category that few mums identify with – Kraft delved deeper. They recognised that mums are multi-dimensional, with the inference in their campaign that just because a mum opts to use a pre-made cheese sauce tonight, it doesn't mean she won't cook a 3 course meal from scratch at the weekend.

As human beings, we are conditioned from an early age to think in binary terms — that is, polarised options involving "either/or", or "all or nothing." When it comes to marketing, however, overgeneralisation is never a good idea, as it ignores the middle ground. This is what makes the tapestry approach so compelling. By concentrating on common threads that mums themselves can identify with (often through self-selection), we no longer think in terms of mums who cook versus mums who don't, but instead, recognise that there may be mums who cook 4 or 5 nights a week, but who rely on takeaways and ready-meals the rest of the time.

Breaking the market into smaller clusters of mums with common identifiable characteristics and needs in this way enables us to do two things: (1) create goods and services that are better tailored to the needs of specific families; and (2) focus our marketing resources more efficiently.

The unsolicited advert that appeared in your Facebook newsfeed from a PR strategist you have never heard of is a perfect example of this form of targeted marketing in action. Based on your recent activity on the platform, Facebook placed you in a tribe of entrepreneurs and business-owners who they think is most receptive to receiving such invitations. Similarly, that advert you saw promoting Kraft macaroni and cheese – that was probably because Facebook knows that you are a parent who likes to use the f-word from time to time.

Social bubbles

Thanks to social media, it is now easier than ever to identify tribes of mums that will likely take an interest in your product or service. Through Facebook groups and other online forums, mums are increasingly filtering themselves into communities based on common characteristics, passions, interests and needs.

Type "mums who" into the search bar in Facebook and you'll find literally thousands of groups covering everything from "mums who lift" to "mums who say

F@#*!!". While I am not suggesting that you structure your entire marketing campaign based on the many different Facebook groups that exist, these groups can be beneficial from a marketing perspective, with the larger and more established groups opening the door to customer collaborations, brand advocacy and word-of-mouth recommendations.

Such communities not only reflect mums' true interests but, more importantly, also connect mums to others with the similar passions. Conversations and interactions within these groups also represent an ideal listening post for brands, enabling us to glean direct "fly on the wall" insights to which we ordinarily might not be privy.

Of course, not all socially-driven tribes will be relevant, and sometimes it will make sense to define your target audience using traditional demographic or socio-economic classifications. For example, if you are in the business of selling a low-involvement product such as school socks, there is not much point in factoring in behavioural and psychographic characteristics. Targeting mums of school-aged children in the economic group most relevant to your price-point would clearly be the most relevant approach in this instance.

However, if your business sells educational games aimed at parents who want to support their children's learning, then a more effective strategy would be to separate mums of school-aged children into tribes and target those most likely to be interested in your products. One approach might be to target mums of school-aged children who have visited a museum with their child and/or mums who belong to their local library, although this is probably easier said than done. Alternatively, you might follow Kraft's lead and hypothesise that mums who regularly bake are more likely to take an active interest in their child's education, which would be an altogether much easier segment to tap into. (Note: just to be clear, I am not suggesting that this is necessarily the case, but rather that it *might* be; as always, I would urge readers to check the validity of such assumptions through independent research before proceeding with any formal marketing strategy).

Going after the right tribes

Once you have identified a few different tribes of mums relevant to your business and confirmed any unsubstantiated claims with research, you need to figure out which tribes represent the greatest profit potential. Factors that you might want to consider include:

- **The number of customers in the tribe and their total spending potential**
  The tribe should contain enough mums with enough spending power to make your

marketing efforts worthwhile. Ideally, the mums in the tribe will be heavy users of whatever you aim to sell. Better still, the number of potential buyers in the tribe should be growing.

- **Your ability to reach customers in the tribe – and the cost of doing so**

  A tribe is not attractive if its members are hard to reach or if the cost of doing so is prohibitively expensive. Mums who have given birth in the Portland, Britain's only private maternity hospital, might seem like an ideal market for a new luxury children's fashion brand. But reaching them is another story, because the hospital protects the privacy of its patients. Similarly, readers of Mother & Baby magazine might appear to be a perfect fit for your new organic baby skincare range, but the cost of ad space in the magazine relative to actual responses and sales revenue might prove prohibitively expensive.

- **The intensity of existing competition in the tribe**

  Start-ups often find that the tribes with the greatest overall profit potential have already been targeted by an army of competitors. For example, the Baby Led Weaning (BLW) community might seem like the ideal launch pad for your new range of sleeved bibs. But with several well-established brands already firmly entrenched in this market, you might want to consider whether you would be better targeting the craft market instead.

- **The level of mums' satisfaction with competitors' current offerings**
  Even when the marketplace is full of products not dissimilar to yours, research may reveal that mums are dissatisfied with current offerings and would welcome something new. On the other hand, if the level of satisfaction with the existing product selection is high, you will likely struggle to gain market share. The infant medicine market is a good example of this, with the level of trust in branded medicines such as Calpol and Nurofen so strong that other brands struggle to get a look-in.

- **Barriers to entry**
  There are many factors outside your control that can make the market less contestable and

less competitive. In the baby-product industry especially, success often requires a product to have a critical mass of users. People don't necessarily buy the safest car seat, but the one they see their friends using. Equally, some brands may be so strong that no amount of advertising may be able to dislodge the incumbent firm. Many firms have tried to enter the nappy cream market, for example, but none have been able to dislodge the much loved brand Sudocrem.

Clearly, there is much to consider when targeting mums, and you should proceed with caution. Many companies think they already understand mums. But most often, they consider only demographic or other overly simplistic factors that merely classify mums into groups, which results in a superficial understanding of mums at best. But as we shall see in the next chapter, when companies truly spend time getting to know their customers based on their less-obvious customer-defined needs and desires, great things happen.

The downside of targeting specific groups of mums is that it limits the number of people who will learn about your product or service. But that is ok. Returning to our tapestry analogy, you need to learn to focus your efforts on the mums who weave their tapestries in strong and vibrant colours that are relevant to your brand. The mums who weave their tapestries in wishy-washy shades of pale cream and grey are not your target audience. That's not to say they never will be – social identities are not static and mums are continually weaving their tapestries. People can add threads, alter the colour of their threads, and weave different colours and designs into their tapestries to reflect the dynamic nature of their identities, likes and dislikes. As they progress through their parenting journey, some threads will become more prominent than others, while others will slowly disappear from view.

For now, you want to concentrate on those who have already identified themselves as being a good fit for your product or service. Recognise that you will never appeal to everyone. Rather than taking a one-size-fits-all approach, fine tune your campaigns based on the threads that are most commonly used by your target market. This will give you a huge advantage over your competitors and enable you to position your product in such a way that it truly stands out in the mind of your customers.

Over to you

Try to identify at least 5 different character traits common to the types of mum who might be interested in your product or service. Try to include a range of demographic, behavioural and attitudinal traits.

"

In the factory we
make cosmetics.
In the store we
sell hope.

"

- Charles Revson

4.

PERFECT POSITIONING

The customer's perception is your reality

Ask Brits to name popular lunchbox snacks, and the chances are they will mention Dairylea. The brand first hit our shelves in 1950, and has successfully maintained its position as the nation's favourite cheese snack ever since.[25] With its impenetrable foil triangles and ensuing squidgy mess, the mere mention of the brand is enough to transport most Brits straight back to their childhood. But just what is it about Dairylea that has enabled the brand to hold onto its place as the UK's top-selling cheese brand for over half a century?[26]

Much of Dairylea's success stems from the fact that it appeals to both parents and their children. As any parent can attest, mums and children have very different ideas about what constitutes a suitable lunchbox snack. While both parties typically agree that every packed lunch should include a sandwich and a drink, opinion is divided over what else should be included. Parents tend to favour a healthy option such as a piece of fruit, whereas kids would rather be given something fun, such as sweets or chocolate. The magic of Dairylea is that through their range of innovatively packaged cheese options and dunk pots, they have managed to come up with something that is considered to be both healthy *and* fun. In other words, they have positioned themselves to appeal to both parents and their children – something that most other food brands can only dream of. Unlike the Kraft Macaroni and Cheese boxes that we described in Chapter 3, parents don't feel any guilt about feeding their children Dairylea. Since they grew up on it themselves, there's a residual element of nostalgia surrounding Dairylea that leads parents to conclude that it is a safe and healthy option to feed to their children.[27]

How do your customers view your brand?

Positioning is all about managing how your customers perceive your product or service. It is what comes to mind when your target market thinks about your brand, products, or services relative to your competitor's offering. What are the benefits of using your brand over other brands? How will using your brand help or enhance your customers' lives? What is it about your brand that makes it so special? What are your brand's strengths and weaknesses, and how do these compare to those of your competitors?

To find your own unique position in the market, you need to identify one or two characteristics of your product or service that will appeal to consumers and word it in such a way that it sticks in their minds. Volvo, for example, is known for producing safe and durable vehicles; Bounty makes absorbent paper towels; Colgate protects against cavities; Weetabix fuels the family; Pampers stay dry; Petits Filous builds strong bones; Duracell makes long-lasting batteries; Fairy is gentle on your hands; Dairylea is full of calcium goodness.

It sounds simple, but in practice, figuring out what separates your product from the rest of the pack and articulating it in a clear and concise way takes time. Add to this the fact that in many cases you must position your product in such a way that it appeals to both parents and their children, and it is clear that positioning is about more than just identifying your product's core strengths.

Identify your opponents

In order to position your product or service effectively, you must first identify your competition. Who are they? It is a simple question, but remember, the real competition – the one that has the potential to kill your business – may not come from a company offering a similar product or service to you, but from a totally different section of the market.

Everyone has heard the cautionary tales of companies like Blockbuster or Kodak, who failed to react to new technologies that dramatically changed their market. With the benefit of hindsight, we can shake our heads and wonder how Blockbuster failed to see that Netflix would forever change the movie rental business, or question why Kodak did not recognise that digital imaging would forever reshape photography.

But this is not the point. The message you should take away from these examples is not that companies like Blockbuster and Kodak lacked foresight, but that competition can come in many different shapes and sizes. Rather than shaking your head in astonishment as Amazon redefines retail, or Uber reshapes transportation, consider the likelihood that a substitute for your product or service could threaten your business in much the same way, and try to think about where such an offering might come from.

To identify your full range of competitors, it is important to consider the problem you are addressing rather than simply focusing on products or services similar to yours. Solutions come in many different forms, and as such, any company that aims to satisfy the same customer needs as yours, may pose a threat. Focus on the brands that mums consider alongside yours – that is, the ones they identify to be your competitors – and not just the ones you think you compete with.

For example, suppose you have developed a board game aimed at helping children learn their times tables. In this instance, your competition comes not just in the form of other board games, but from any product or service that aims to help your child master their times tables. This includes books, worksheets, CDs, online tutorial programs, private tutors, after-school education providers such as Kumon and Kip McGrath, as well as any other tool that innovative education enthusiasts can dream up.

Similarly, if you are in the market of selling festival-friendly pushchairs, you need to consider the relative strengths and weaknesses of your brand compared not just to other pushchair brands, but also to slings, baby carriers, bicycle trailers, utility carts, and anything else that helps get your child from A to B with minimum fuss.

Once you have identified current and potential competitors, the next step is to look at their objectives. If their objectives are very different from yours, you may not need to worry about them. But if your competitors' objectives put them in head-to-head competition with you, the best solution is to try to find a way to differentiate your offer (either through redesign or marketing), or target a different group of mums. The goal here is to stake out a position that makes you less vulnerable to attack from head-to-head opponents (whether established or new), and less vulnerable to erosion from the direction of buyers, suppliers and substitute goods.

Positioning based on hope and fear

One company who understands the importance of positioning better than most is Quidel. Prior to branching out into the home pregnancy test market in the 1990s, Quidel were best known for their in-doctor's-office diagnostic tests, where they had almost an 80 percent share of the $6 million US market.[28] But when Steven Frankel joined the organisation as chief executive in 1992, he decided to expand into the consumer market by introducing a new range of pregnancy and ovulation tests designed to be used at home.

The first step was to look at how existing pregnancy tests were being marketed to consumers. This is when Quidel marketers noticed a problem with the market: the tests were being sold as a single offering that had to appeal to both those who hoped that they were pregnant, as well as those who hoped they weren't. In other words, the tests were positioned in such a way as to try to appeal to as many customers as possible.

It's what marketers often refer to as the *lukewarm tea syndrome*. Some customers prefer hot tea, and some prefer iced tea, which leads some hypothetical marketers to offer lukewarm tea in the hope that it will appeal to both. They later discover that the strategy is flawed when customers head off in search of a product that better matches their needs.

Keen to avoid serving lukewarm tea, the Quidel team realised that they could differentiate themselves by segmenting the market into those who want to be pregnant versus those who don't – and then offering a separate proposition to each. The product would remain the same, but they could customise the packaging, promotion and even the price to appeal to the two different groups of women. Same kit, same technology, different outlook.

By segmenting the market into just two distinct categories like this, the Quidel team uncovered a huge opportunity to target women on both sides of the binary division. At one end of the spectrum sits the positive hopefuls, a group of women hoping to find they are pregnant, while at the other end sits those hoping for a negative result, who we shall call the negative hopefuls. The two groups can be summarised as follows:

➢ *The positive hopefuls:* Full of optimism and hope for the future, the women in this group are excited about the prospect of having a baby. They are happy to shop for a pregnancy test, and might even tell their family and friends that they are taking the test. They feel content when they see baby products on the shelves, and hope that they will soon have reason to shop in this section of the store.

> *The negative hopefuls:* the women who make up this group don't want to be pregnant. They feel nervous buying a pregnancy test, and avoid looking at baby products, not wishing to be reminded that they might be facing an unplanned pregnancy. They typically keep their pregnancy thoughts private, and are hoping for a negative result.

Before reading any further, consider how you might market pregnancy tests to these two very different groups of women.

- How would you name the two different pregnancy tests?

- Is it conceivable that one of the groups might be willing to pay more for the test than the other?

- Where on the shelf might you want to position the product for the positive hopefuls versus the one aimed at the negative hopefuls?

- How might the packaging vary between the two products?

Quidel decided to name the pregnancy test aimed at the positive hopefuls *Conceive*. They packaged the product in a pink and blue box, with the smiling face of a cherubic infant on the front. It could typically be found on a shelf in the baby products aisle, and cost $9.99.

The test aimed at the negative hopefuls, by contrast, was called *RapidVue*. It was packaged in a small, discreet and clinical-looking box, designed to be barely noticeable in the shopping basket. There were no pictures of smiling babies on the box, and it certainly didn't look out of place next to the condoms and other contraceptive products that sat alongside it on the shelf. Price: $6.99.

It is interesting to note that Quidel created these two clearly defined brands without changing the core product at all. The contents of the boxes were to all intents and purposes, identical. Yet to consumers, the products appeared totally different. The positive hopefuls felt happy when they saw a beautiful baby smiling back at them from the box, while the negative hopefuls appreciated being able to buy a low-key package that promised quick results at a relatively cheap price. Neither segment felt as though they were being served lukewarm tea. Two different propositions for two very different segments.

What is remarkable about this story is that it was Quidel's first foray into the business-to-consumer (B2C) market. Despite having no prior experience of marketing directly to consumers, they were able to position their products in a way that none of their competitors had thought of. Their strategy clearly paid off, with Quidel managing to grow its home pregnancy test sales to $4 million in a total market of $20 million in less than three years.[29]

Features tell, benefits sell

Choosing how to position your product or service is one of the most important decisions you will make and it is imperative that you get it right. Fail to position your product or service in mums' minds, and you risk others – including your competitors – doing it for you.

There are several factors to consider when identifying your unique position in the market.

- **Product features**
  Is there something about your product or service that makes it seem better or different than your competition?

- **Rational benefits**
  What do mums get out of buying or using your product or service?

- **Emotional benefits**
  How does using your product or service make mums feel?

FIGURE 4-1: Rational versus emotional benefits

PRODUCT FEATURES What do you do?	RATIONAL BENEFITS What do I get?	EMOTIONAL BENEFITS How do I feel?
MumVit is a multi-vitamin formulated just for mums	MumVit gives you the energy to power through the day	MumVit will leave you feeling refreshed and able to keep up with your kids from morning to night
Family Bank stays open until 10pm	Family Bank fits in with your schedule instead of you having to fit in with theirs	With Family Bank, you will spend less time worrying about your finances, and more time doing the things you love
Helfee Cereal is a great tasting low calorie cereal	By eating Helfee cereal once a day, you can lose up to a stone in six weeks	Helfee Cereal will put you in control of your weight and have you feeling fabulous in no time at all

The emotional benefits of your brand should not be overlooked. Most people are better at identifying the rational benefits of their product or service than they are at identifying the emotional benefits. However, if you want to make your brand a success, it is essential that you learn to appeal to mums' hearts as much as to their minds. Stop telling mums what you do and start telling them what they get and how it will make them feel.

Ideally, the word or phrase you come up with should be unique to your brand. Nobody has managed to shift the perception of Volvo as the "safe" car, or Duracell as the "long-lasting" battery, and similarly, you shouldn't try to position your product in a space that has previously been claimed by one of your competitors either.

Try to think about the single most compelling and persuasive reason why mums would purchase your product or service over one of your competitors' products. This reason is your "promise" to customers; it is the essence of your value proposition.

Next, consider what evidence can you offer to make your product's point of difference believable. The product's functional, economic, and/or emotional attributes must be credible to assure customers that the brand will deliver on its promise. The reason to believe is something that is inherent in the product or your company that customers associate with your ability to deliver the promised point of difference. How does Direct Line offer competitive car insurance? By cutting out the middleman. Why does John Lewis offer value for money? Because they are "never knowingly undersold."

Keep in mind that the goal of positioning is not to come up with a clever tagline, but rather to identify a simple phrase or concept that you want to get into the head of your target customer. A positioning statement is a statement of strategy, outlining how you wish your brand to be perceived by those outside your organisation. It is not designed to be used as an advertising slogan, but rather a guide that can be used to shape your marketing messages. Think of it as a blueprint for how you want mums to view your product/service/brand relative to competitors. Remember this and your positioning has a chance to be adopted by the mums you are aiming to serve.

Over to you

How do you want your customers to feel about you, every time they think about you? Try to capture that in a brief statement that best describes what you can offer, both in terms of rational and emotional benefits. It might help you to think of it as a sentence where you simply fill in the blanks, such as the following:

For mums who [target market]_____ ,

We provide [rational benefit] _____ ,

Because [proof points] _____ ,

So that [emotional benefit] _____ .

"

The two most
important requirements
for major success are:
first, being in the right
place at the right time,
and second, doing
something about it.

"

- Ray Kroc

5.

HOPE IS NOT A STRATEGY

A great product is wonderful, but it's not a business model

In the film *Field of Dreams*, Kevin Costner plays an Iowan farmer called Ray who has fallen on hard times.[30] While walking in his cornfield one night, he hears a voice telling him, "If you build it he will come". In his mind's eye he sees the cornfield transformed into a baseball diamond. Ignoring the pleas of his wife and children, Ray transforms his cornfield into a baseball pitch, and sure enough, "they" come.

The story makes for a great movie, but when applied to business, the idea that "if you build it, they will come" rarely works, particularly when it comes to marketing to mums. Mums aren't waiting for you to save them. Mums are busy people. They're not sitting around searching for the next great parenting hack. But, approach them with a solution to something they are currently struggling with, and deliver it in a way that requires little effort on their part, and you might just win them over.

The four elements of success

When we think of new products, we tend to think of them as being built for existing markets. But the reality is, every product requires its own market, which needs to be developed and nurtured along with the product. You can't build something and expect a market to come to you; you have to make mums (or their kids) aware of your product or service and give them a reason to come to you.

Marketing is all about putting the right product in the right place, at the right price, at the right time. Though this sounds like an easy enough proposition, a lot of hard work and research needs to go into making sure this happens. If just one element misses the mark, a promising product or service can fail completely and end up costing a business substantially.

You might already be familiar with the "four Ps" of marketing: product, price, place, and promotion. In order for a product to succeed, each of these elements must be scrutinised and evaluated. No single "P" can be considered in isolation, with each of the four elements contributing to success. You can't develop a product or service without thinking about how to make people aware of its existence. Similarly, charge the wrong price and even the best product or service will fail.

In essence, the 4Ps of marketing is a framework through which to capture the best strategies. The starting point in any marketing plan must always be to identify your target market and come up with a compelling positioning statement that will stick in mums' minds. Once you have done this, the next step is to shape all this into a brilliant 4P strategy that reflects mums' needs, while differentiating you from your competitors, at a price that makes sense to customers.

FIGURE 5-1: The 4Ps of marketing

PRODUCT   PLACE

TARGET GROUP
OF MUMS

PROMOTION   PRICE

The First P: Product

The product (or service) sits at the centre of all your marketing activities. Whether it's a trust fund, a pushchair, or a nursery-school place, the product is defined as whatever it is that you are offering to customers. This includes both tangible and intangible elements. The tangible, of course, are those things that the customer can see, touch, feel, taste, or smell. The intangible factors include such things as quality, durability, ease of use, and after-sales maintenance and repair. In short, the product is the entire package that you offer to customers – that is, the sum of all these elements.

When thinking about the product or service you are offering, it is important to start with the needs of the customer or end-user. New products begin with the customer and their needs, not with a patent, a raw material, or a skill. Rather than focusing on selling your product or service, think about how you can attract mums to your business by providing customer-creating and customer-satisfying propositions. Concentrate on offering things that will make mums want to do business with you, rather than the other way round.

Getting feedback on whether the basic product you are offering to mums hits the right mark is relatively straightforward. But what about the less obvious, more intangible elements of your product or service? How much importance do mums place on these? One approach

FIGURE 5-2: The complete product model

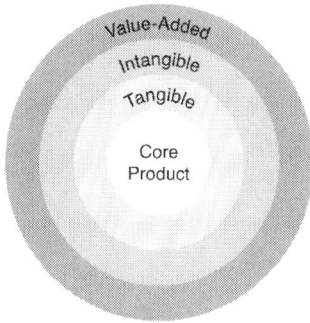

- Does your core product reflect the needs of the end user?

- Do the tangible elements of your product appeal to mums (and if applicable, their children)?

- How much importance do you and your target market place on the intangible elements of your product or service?

- How can you add value and "wow" mums with your knowledge and expertise?

is to use something called the complete product model,[31] separating all the elements of a product or service into four distinct categories as in Fig 5-2.

1) **Core product**

This is the product or service you are offering in its simplest form. Think about the needs of the mums you aim to serve, and if you are targeting more than one type of mum, consider whether it is worth creating separate options for each segment. This will keep you from watering down your offering to something that averages the needs of many mums rather than catering to a tighter group of mums, and will help you avoid the temptation to serve the dreaded lukewarm tea that we discussed earlier. This is a strategy frequently employed by baby food manufacturers, among others. Products with expensive organic ingredients are marketed as premium brands, while those made with standard ingredients are targeted towards the less-affluent, value-oriented mum.

2) **Tangible Elements**

These include packaging, and other physical attributes. Packaging, in particular, is a popular source of differentiation, since it can be more easily modified than actual physical products. Consider, for example, the way Quidel, who we discussed in Chapter 4, packaged their pregnancy tests to appeal to two very different customer segments: same product, different packaging for two very different types of consumer.

3) **Intangible Elements**

These include service components such as warranties, maintenance agreements, delivery and installation speeds, ease of ordering, and trade-in deals. A bike company, for example, might introduce a buy-back scheme that enables parents to trade-in their child's bicycle when he or she outgrows it. Such schemes serve as a powerful marketing tool, encouraging some families to spend more money than they originally planned, safe in the knowledge that some of the money they are spending can be recouped at a later date.

4) **Value-Added Benefits**
This is the provision of added benefits that increase the value of your product in the eyes of mums. The key is to offer strong value that the customer believes exceeds your price point. Often, this involves the use of partners to provide buyers with an additional product or service offering. Children's magazines, for example, often come with a free toy, while family cereals might be accompanied by a voucher entitling the purchaser to a personalised bowl or spoon, or a money-off voucher to an attraction like Legoland. Don't be fooled into thinking that this is something only applicable to large brands, however. One of the most innovative value-added benefits that I have seen in recent years took the form of a paper clothing tag embedded with seeds that could be planted in the garden to leave behind nothing but pretty flowers. The company behind this innovative idea? A kitchen-table business run by a mum of two, with a turnover of less than £50k per year.

The Second P: Place

When it comes to selling to mums, developing a compelling new product is only part of the battle. Ensuring mums are aware of the product and can access it without too much effort can be just as critical to new product success.

Some experts have even gone so far as to suggest that placement and mode of engagement is more important than the core product offering. "Why, if your favourite restaurant is so good, have you not eaten there more often than at, say, Wagamama or McDonald's," was the question Rory Sutherland, Vice Chairman of Ogilvy UK, posed to readers of his column in Campaign magazine.[32] "It is my opinion that the ease and choice of delivery mechanism makes more difference to us (and quality of product far less difference) than we ever care to admit."

Although one might argue that price is a big factor behind us not eating in our favourite restaurants more often, Mr Sutherland does raise an interesting point. People don't go to Starbucks and KFC for the quality of the food, but because of the convenience they offer, and the flexibility of delivery. Similarly, few of us routinely go to flea-markets or car boot sales, but we will buy from Facebook selling pages or eBay, even though we don't typically get to see what we are buying before parting with our cash. Argos, with their "Ring & Reserve" and "Click & Collect" options is another example of a great success being pioneered on the back of the mode of delivery rather than the intrinsic merits of the offering. Compare the Market is another.

Certainly, when faced with a choice between spending an hour travelling to a shopping mall to buy the perfect gift for their child, or spending less than 5 minutes ordering an inferior version on Amazon, many mums have no qualms about opting for the latter. It's no coincidence that mums are the primary users of Amazon Prime in the UK, with as many as one in three British families currently subscribing to the service.[33] The main reason? According to a recent IOM survey of Amazon Prime users, it's the promise of free next-day delivery that coaxes most mums into joining, with very few taking advantage of the additional benefits that the service offers, such as TV and movie streaming.[34]

Regardless of which channels you decide to sell your products through, the chances are you will need to spend a significant amount of time on market development. While popular e-commerce sites such as Amazon and eBay offer access to a large number of mums, you need to do more than simply list your product on one of these platforms to get your product seen. There are over 150 million different products for sale on Amazon.co.uk, and as such, it takes more than a selection of images and a "buy it now" button to get mums to even find – let alone buy – your product.[35]

While online is now responsible for as much as half of all purchases made by mums in the UK, it is important not to put all your eggs in one basket. Few successful companies rely on just one single place through which to sell their products, and you shouldn't either. There are many different paths to mums, and as such, you should aim to take advantage of as many of them as you can reasonably handle, without causing conflict between channels.

The Third P: Promotion

Promotion is all about how you communicate your market position to ensure that mums know about your product or service, have a favourable impression of it, and ultimately, decide that they need it in their lives. It includes elements such as TV, radio and print advertising, public relations, social media marketing, email marketing, direct sales, customer loyalty schemes, two-for-one dinner specials, and so on.

The secret to great promotion lies in having a detailed strategic marketing plan in place before starting to think about creative advertising opportunities. Before thinking about how you can use social media (or any tactic for that matter) to connect with mums, take a step back and ensure that your overall strategy is defined. Your strategy sets out your vision and goals, and determines where to play and how to win in the marketplace. Think of promotion as a tactic employed to deliver on that strategy. It's an important part of the marketing plan, but it's certainly not the starting point.

The Fourth P: Price

Last but not least is pricing. You don't want to undermine your strategy by leaving money on the table, but equally, you don't want to get overly greedy and alienate the very mums you are trying to reach.

When setting their prices, many businesses use a cost-plus-pricing approach, adding an arbitrary margin to the amount it costs them to produce or manufacture their product. There are a couple of advantages to this approach – not least its simplicity, and the fact that it is extremely easy to compute. The downside is that it fails to take into consideration the actual value that is being offered to the customer, and as such, often results in products being sold for less than the customer might otherwise have been prepared to pay.

An altogether better strategy therefore, is to set your pricing based on the intrinsic value being offered to purchasers. At the upper end, you are bound by mums' perceived value for the product, as influenced by the company's marketing effort to communicate the product's benefits, as well as by the price of alternative products on offer. At the lower end, you are bound by the cost of producing the product. By pricing above the cost of production, and below perceived value, you have an incentive to sell the product, while the purchaser has an incentive to buy.

Consider, for example, the incredible success of Fever-Tree, a premium tonic water brand that launched in the UK in 2005. Despite costing over three times as much as Schweppes tonic water, Fever-Tree has managed to capture a quarter of the entire UK mixer market by using their pricing as a differentiator in a strategy has helped them position themselves as a drink for those with sophisticated tastes.[36] The drinks comes in sleek glass bottles to help justify their premium price, and the flavours are fancy too. "Elderflower Tonic Water," "Spiced Orange Ginger Ale" and "Premium Indian Tonic Water" are just a few of the offerings. "If 3/4 of your gin & tonic is TONIC, make sure you use THE BEST," scream Fever-Tree advertisements in magazines and train stations across the country.

Of course, when thinking about the value that mums place on your product, it is important to recognise that value, like beauty, is in the eye of the beholder. Not all mums will see the value in spending £3.40 for a litre of tonic water, when they could pick up a supermarket's own branded one for as little as 40p. In much the same way, mums who go camping with their kids would likely place much more value in a camera-phone with a waterproof hard-wearing case than those who don't. As such, when thinking about how much to charge for your product or service, you should be very clear about which group of mums you plan to target, and conduct your research accordingly.

Over to you

Consider how the 4Ps connect with each other in the context of your business or brand, and think about how you can deliver additional value. What elements of your 4P marketing strategy do you need to improve?

"

People will forget what
you said, people will forget
what you did, but people
will never forget how you
made them feel.

"

- Maya Angelou

6.

BUILDING A BRAND MUMS TRUST

A brand is more than just a pretty face

When I talk to start-ups and small businesses about their branding, they often tell me that they have it covered. They typically mean that they have a name, a logo, and a nice website in place. Lots of people think that brand begins and ends there — that once they have a catchy name and a swanky logo that they can stick below their email signature and on their website, they have a brand. Much of my work consists of disabusing people of this notion.

Brand is your strategy. It is the products and services that you offer, and the story behind them. Ikea's warehouses and commitment to keeping costs down is its brand. Comic Relief's mission to end childhood poverty by encouraging people to cast their inhibitions aside and raise money for charity on Red Nose Day is its brand. Ryanair's PR stunts such as claims the airline is considering introducing "standing seats" on their planes and charging passengers to use the on-board toilets is its brand.[37]

Brand is your customer service. It is about how you deal with complaints and whether you are prepared to go the extra mile for your customers and take ownership of your mistakes when things go wrong. Mothercare sending a box of discontinued shoes to a boy with Autism is its brand.[38] Graco reaching out to mums on social media to explain why it was necessary to recall millions of car seats is its brand.[39] A coffee shop refusing a mum hot water to heat her baby's bottle is its brand.[40]

Brand is the way you communicate with your customers. If you patronise mums, that's your brand. If you use acronyms and industry jargon that is difficult to comprehend, that's your brand. If you're trying to be all things to all people, that's also your brand. Similarly, if a member of staff spends more time joking around with his colleagues than serving customers, he's your brand, whether he's got your company logo emblazoned across his chest or not.

Brand is the technology that drives your sales. If your website's functionality isn't up to scratch, or if it's slow to load and frustrating to use, that's your brand. If people can't get in touch with you on the telephone, or get passed from pillar to post, or end up spending 20 minutes listening to canned music, that's your brand. Amazon's ease of ordering through its 1-Click button is its brand.

Brand is the space between expectation and reality. How many times have you encountered a product or service that didn't live up to its promises? That disconnect is your brand. Asda's decision to substitute a cuddly toy for a roast chicken in a customer's online order is its brand.[41] That McDonald's hamburgers look nothing like they do in the pictures is its brand.

Brand is what customers think of when they hear your company's name. This includes your logo and colour palette, your choice of artwork and font, the quality and sustainability of your packaging, but it also includes so much more. It is everything that your customers and prospective customers think, feel, say, hear, read, watch, imagine and even hope about your product, service or organisation.

What does your brand say to mums?

Whether you have a swanky logo or not, you have a brand. The question is whether the brand you *have* and the brand you *want to have* are one and the same thing. You might have a professionally-printed sales banner that perfectly complements your website, but if it's pinned up with duct tape and sagging in the middle, that becomes your brand. It tells customers you don't pay attention to detail. Can you imagine seeing a crooked banner with duct tape in an Apple store? Never. And that's their brand. It says that the motherboard in the Mac isn't hanging by a thread either.

Ultimately, brand is about caring about your business at every level and in every detail, from the big things like the products you sell to the mums you are trying to sell to and every interaction they are ever going to have with your brand. The people who buy and use your products form part of your brand, too, and as such, it is important to think about what message they are sending out to prospective leads and how they fit in with your overall brand strategy.

This last point should not be overlooked. Whether you like it or not, your brand will always be judged by outsiders based on your existing customers. A school might have an excellent rating from Ofsted, but if the most visible aspect of the school to outsiders is the large gaggle of parents who stand outside the school gates smoking, then it will never be as appealing to a certain demographic of mums as the school round the corner where the kids are dropped off in high-end Audis and BMWs.

One brand that understands the importance of making sure their existing customers align with their brand identity is Abercrombie & Fitch. The teen clothing brand recently reversed the normal rules of product endorsement by offering a "substantial" sum to Michael Sorrentino – AKA The Situation from MTV's Jersey Shore – not to wear its clothes, claiming that the show's cocktail of sex, alcohol, bragging and bad behaviour did not fit in with the brand's aspirational image, and might put off some parents from buying the clothes for their children.[42]

As extreme as this sounds, much of Abercrombie and Fitch's success lies in their uncompromising approach to targeting. In an interview with Salon, CEO Mike Jeffries explained the logic behind their strategy. "The companies that are in trouble are trying to target everybody: young, old, fat, skinny. They don't alienate anybody, but they don't excite anybody, either. Candidly, we go after the cool kids – the attractive all-American kid with a great attitude and a lot of friends. Are we exclusionary? Absolutely."[43]

While I don't advocate paying people not to use your products, it is important to stay on top of who is buying your product and how they fit in with in with your overall brand image. All too often, companies get stuck in a "we" mindset: How *we* want our brand to be portrayed. What *we* think the strengths of our products or services are. Who *we* think should buy our brand. The key to building a successful brand is recognising that it is never about us, and always about them – the customer. Be honest with yourself about who your customers actually are (and not just who you think they are, or worse, who you would like them to be), and use them to shape your strategy accordingly.

Connect and communicate

When marketing to mums, it is important that you are open and honest about your brand's mission, vision, and values. Propositions should be authentic and tie directly back to brand values, and faithfully express brand personality. Building trust is crucial to a brand, therefore interactions with customers should be authentic and consistently demonstrate whatever it is about your brand that you consider to be important and worthwhile. Without this consistency, mums won't know what to expect and will question the authenticity of your brand.

It's not enough to simply offer great products. You need to compel mums to do business with you by making a connection with their lives, their needs and desires, and drawing them towards you and your brand story. You have to give them a reason to bundle the kids into their car seats and drive across town to purchase your product instead of just going online and buying a generic – and probably cheaper – equivalent elsewhere. To do this, you need to drill deeper into their psyche and understand what you're really selling, why it matters and how you can enrich the lives of the families you are ultimately targeting. Think about your brand purpose and how best to communicate this to your target market. While making money is important to almost every business, mums admire brands that are able to demonstrate a willingness to achieve more than just profitability.

Successful brands seek to entice, inspire and engage prospects, rather than simply pushing their products and services. Take Swedish retailer Ikea, for example. Their vision isn't just to sell furniture, but rather, to "create a better everyday life." While this may sound like little more than clever copy, the company is very good at inspiring customers by creating engaging and interesting content that keeps their customers coming back for more. A few years ago, for example, Ikea conducted a phone survey of 1,000 adults and found that 72 percent think that a stressful morning affects the rest of their day, and 75 percent don't have a regular morning routine. In response to this, the company launched the *First: 59* campaign, with a website featuring tips and tricks on how to make the 59 minutes of your day as smooth as possible.[44] With emphasis on how to improve organisation, utility and comfort in the bedroom and bathroom, the website is structured around chunks of knowledge from four lifestyle and design experts and bloggers, and includes everything from getting the kids ready on time to finding your wallet and phone.

Another great way to bring mums on board and keep them engaged and loyal to your brand is to build a community around your product. The genius of this approach is that instead of trying to persuade mums that they *need* your product and perpetuating an 'us-them' relationship, you're dissolving boundaries and forming a 'we' experience. You're opening the door, welcoming them in for coffee, inviting feedback and offering them a space where they can interact with like-minded individuals.

One brand that is particularly good at recognising the importance of nurturing and supporting their brand communities is Lego. What could be more enticing to a Lego enthusiast than having their design idea on the shelves – and being awarded a percentage of the product sales? This is the idea behind Lego Ideas, which invites Lego fans from around the world to submit ideas, offer feedback, and vote for the designs they would like to see turned into official Lego sets. Championing creativity, this initiative rewards loyal customers and gives them a reason to invest in the brand.

Never underestimate the power of a good story, either. Telling your story is a critical part of building your brand. It helps to shape how people view you and enables consumers to begin forging a connection with your company. Do it right, and you'll put building blocks in place that will allow you to develop a strong brand that people buy from simply because they love what you do and what you stand for.

Isla Rowntree, founder of Islabikes, is a great example of a founder who understands the importance of storytelling in building a strong brand. At the centre of the company is a well-spun tale – one in which a former competitive cyclist becomes frustrated with the cheap, heavy, poorly designed, uncomfortable bikes that her sister's children were struggling to enjoy and decides to design her own range of kids' bikes. It's an authentic story, and one that resonates with parents.

"If you took an adult's body and just scaled it down, you wouldn't have something that looked like a child's body," explains Ms Rowntree. "For example, a small child's head is much bigger relative to its body than an adult's. We design our bikes around children's proportions, factoring in not just height, leg length and weight but also a vast range of things you might never think of such as hand strength, foot size, hand width, grip diameter etc."[45]

Ms Rowntree claims she didn't set out to run a global business. She just wanted to change the way kids' bikes were made, which she has done very successfully. The brand has no distinctive logo to speak of, there are no catchy slogans on the company website, they don't have a strong social media presence, and at the time of writing, the bikes are only available through the Islabikes website.

And yet Islabikes holds the enviable position as market leader of children's bicycles, which has been achieved almost exclusively through word-of-mouth marketing based on little more than a powerful back story a commitment to helping children master bike-riding as quickly and efficiently as possible.

Children's footwear company Start-rite is another example of a brand that understands the importance of building narrative into their branding. Founded in 1792, the company was the first shoemaker in Britain to introduce ready-made off-the-shelf shoes for children in variable width fittings. Over two centuries later, and their mission remains the same: to supply good quality footwear that enables your child's feet to grow healthily while complementing their lifestyle.

"We do a lot of research into what actually happens to children's feet and how children live and move," explains CEO Ian Watson.[46] "Girls are playing as much football as boys and are just as tough on their shoes, so we need to ensure we cater for that. Forest schools are also a big trend, where the focus is on learning through outdoor play, so our products have to reflect this changing market."

To remind customers of their commitment to making sure that their shoes are robust and meet the needs of today's children, Start-rite recently refreshed their branding, making sure that activity and movement figured more heavily in their website images and in their advertising campaigns, all the while paying homage to the brand's rich heritage. "It's about evolving the brand to make it more relevant for today's market," said Watson. "Evolution rather than revolution."

A brand by any other name

Whether you're starting a new company or overhauling the image of an existing one, building a brand is a big undertaking with extremely high stakes. Getting your brand wrong as a start-up means failing to resonate with your target audience. Messing up a rebranding or repositioning effort as an established firm could mean alienating and ultimately losing your loyal customer base.

In the end, the strength of a brand comes down to distinction – namely your ability to set your brand apart from others in your industry through the eyes of your customers. If the mums you are targeting truly value the difference that sets your products and services apart from rival offerings, they will either 1) select your brand over others, 2) be willing to pay a premium for what you are offering, or 3) act on a combination of 1 and 2. Loyal Nike fans won't purchase a pair of Adidas trainers even if they're on sale, in much the same way that fans of a particular coffee shop will walk 3 extra blocks past several other coffee outlets in order to satiate their morning coffee fix.

Of course, sometimes being different simply means being better. Plenty of mums don't want bells and whistles and other differentiators as much as they want simple to use, quality products, reliable service, on-time delivery and fair value for money. If you can deliver on these requirements better than others, you may have all the differentiation you need to be successful.

Over to you

Using the questions on page 87 as a guide, think about how you might go about describing your brand to an external agency or investor. Try to keep your answers as succinct as possible, and avoid any use of jargon.

STRATEGIC BRAND BUILDING QUESTIONS

1. **What does your business / product do?**
   If you had just 30 seconds to explain your product to a customer, what would you say?

2. **What is your mission?**
   What problem do you solve for your customers? What is the purpose of your company's existence (other than to make money)?

3. **How does your branding differ from that of your 3 main competitors?**
   What do you like and dislike about your competitors' brands? Know who you are competing against and learn from them, but don't copy them. Do your own thing.

4. **What about your background or product or service sets you apart from your competitors?**
   Why should your prospects buy from you or engage with you? What makes your company different?

5. **Is there a unique story behind your business or business name or logo?**
   People connect through stories. Storytelling is a great way to create and sell a brand image. What's yours?

6. **What 5 adjectives best describe your brand?**
   Ask your colleagues for their input. Then ask your customers. Are the words that you come up with similar? If not, why not?

66

Social media is about sociology and psychology more than technology.

99

- Brian Solis

7.

LET'S GET SOCIAL

(But not too social)

Let's be honest, many of us spend too much time on social media. And mums are no exception. Research released by Facebook shows mums are the site's most active group of users, over-indexing on every activity except one – the check-in. First-time mums with infants under the age of two are especially active on social media, with new mothers launching their first Facebook session at 4:00am, on average, reaching peak activity at 7:00am, according to Facebook official data. [47]

For many mums, it would seem that feeding time is quite literally, Facebook time. This provides companies with an enormous opportunity to reach out to new mums and introduce them to their products and services –

particularly if your target market is under the age of 35. According to Facebook, mums aged 18-34 are three times more likely to share photos and fives times more likely to share videos than non-mums of the same age.

But while social media can be a great tool for brands looking for ways to connect with mums and introduce them to their products and services, it is important to maintain perspective, and see social media for what it is: just another channel through which to disseminate your message. As effective as social media can be at enabling marketers to reach large numbers of people with relatively little financial outlay, social media cannot and should not replace your overall marketing strategy, and instead, should be integrated into your wider marketing activities to support and enhance your overall strategic goals, objectives and outcomes.

One of the downsides of the rise of Facebook as a marketing vehicle is that it has spawned a generation of young professionals who talk instead of listen. They think engaging in "the conversation" is more important than identifying their audience, understanding what motivates them, and developing powerful messaging to address those motivations. This is a mistake. Social media is not a magic bullet for new sales. It never has been, and it never will be. It's just one of many available platforms for your marketing message, and should be used as such.

By all means leverage social media to gain mums' trust,

but don't rely on it as the major focus of your marketing efforts. In other words, don't exclude social media, be present there, but make use of other marketing tactics and tools as well.

And above all, don't be disheartened if your social media following doesn't grow as quickly as you might like. Remember, mums typically use social media during their down-time as a form of relaxation and a way to connect with their family and friends. Rarely do they purposefully seek out brands on social media, and as such, the more inward-facing your brand is on social media, the slower your growth will be. Having said that, it is important not to lose sight of why you are on social media, and not to dilute your brand with too many funny memes and links to external content just because you think it will generate lots of likes and shares. As with anything, it is all about balance, and finding what works best for you and your target market.

With that in mind, here are my top ten tips for building a social media presence that mums will be happy to follow and engage with:

1. Become an authority
Today's mums aren't so different from their mums, or even their mums' mums. They have many of the same parenting questions, and they experience similar joys. But the resources they use to manage the complexities of

motherhood have changed. This presents a very real opportunity for brands to connect with mums on social media by offering their advice and tips on a particular aspect of parenting relevant to their area of expertise.

Breast pump brand Medela is a good example of a company that has built up a loyal following on social media by providing insightful content and useful feeding tips to mums. The company regularly posts content on their pages covering everything from how to pump milk while studying at university to what foods to eat to help stimulate milk supply and help balance hormones. The brand also runs a live Q&A session with an in-house lactation consultant on their UK Facebook page once a week, where mums can seek advice in real-time.

2. Share relevant and interesting third party content, but not at the expense of your own content

Sharing informative content from trusted third-party sources is a great way to let mums know who you are and what you stand for. However, post too much external content, and you risk diluting your overall message. A good rule of thumb is to share at most, one piece of third-party content for every 3 or 4 pieces of original content. This could be a newspaper article about a new trend affecting your industry, a humorous or tongue-in-cheek picture of a mum who looks like she could benefit from using your product, or even a critical review in which you acknowledge your shortcomings. The point is that there are other things happening around your customers and their families that involve you and your brand, and third-party content can help you connect with them in their world.

BigJigs Toys is a lovely example of a company that has got its social media strategy spot on. Turn to their Facebook page, and you will see a mixture of posts showcasing their own products in engaging and sometimes entertaining ways, alongside newspaper and blog posts discussing wider trends relevant to their customers, and a few humorous memes thrown in for good measure. Although the page doesn't have the largest following, their level of engagement is good (meaning that mums regularly read, like, share and comment on their posts), and the balance of posts is such that parents who happen across the page by chance won't be left in any doubt as to what the brand stands for, and what sort of products they sell.

3. Monitor and offer support

Mums are far more likely to trust brands on social media who are helpful and actively engage with their audience than those who don't. This means commenting and answering questions, responding to messages in a timely fashion, and generally being present. Monitor your social media platforms for tags and mentions, and conduct regular searches for the name of your company, products, services, and URLs, too. Mums often mention brands in conversations without tagging them, so don't just rely on popup notifications within your social media apps to monitor what is being said about you.

While you should answer all questions you can on social, it's not possible all the time. Not everything can be solved in 140 characters or less, and that's okay—it's perfectly acceptable to send people to a more appropriate channel, such as a customer support email address or phone number. You're still being helpful by redirecting them to a platform where they'll get their question answered quickly and efficiently.

4. Show there are people behind your brand

Your followers aren't interacting with robots on social media—they're interacting with people. Show them this. Sometimes the easiest and most effective social content are behind-the-scenes snapshots and content that offers the consumer an intimate experience of the brand, taking them where they would otherwise not have access to explore, and giving them a first-hand view of the lives of those behind the brand. If you're running a competition, for example, consider posting photos of the prizes being packaged up and prepared for shipping. It will help reassure mums that the competition is genuine, and help generate buzz.

5. Avoid click-bait headlines

Don't fall back on click-bait formats for your headlines that you think will draw clicks. You need to strike a balance between writing clear, concise headlines, and being emotionally evocative. You don't want someone to click on your message and then find that your content doesn't deliver.

6. Don't be afraid to experiment

Every brand is different, and what works for one of your competitors might not be right for you and your audience. Experiment by posting different content at different times, and see what gets the best reaction from your fans. Don't get too hung up on the frequency of your posts, either. While some brands like to be seen to be posting content on their social media platforms every few minutes, others, like Apple, don't even bother with social media at all. Don't fall into the trap of posting for the sake of posting. If in doubt, remember that nobody ever decided to unfollow a social media account because they were posting too little!

7. Learn to speak the language of each platform, and think carefully before deciding where to play

Imagine showing up to a party where everyone appears to be speaking German. Now imagine trying to tell a story in Portuguese. Chances are you'd lose your fellow partygoers' interest pretty fast. The same goes when posting content on social media that doesn't suit the personality of the platform. You wouldn't want to share a serious, text-heavy message on a highly visual platform like Instagram, for example. Similarly, where Twitter's character limit dictates that text is kept punchy and directive, longer-form or more narrative-based captions often work better on personal relationship networks like Facebook. Keep your content on the mark by tailoring your message to the tone of each platform, and understanding the different ways that mums use social media. Don't try to be too ambitious either. Being everywhere on social media is not a great business strategy. Being relevant and successful on just one or two major platforms will always trump being lacklustre everywhere.

8. Self-promote the right way

Social media is a great medium for promoting your content, products, and services, but you have to do it the right way. Don't be overly salesy or pushy. Provide helpful, valuable content and show your brand personality by using positive language. Make it easy to share, or better yet, make it fun to share by coming up with fresh and innovative ways to frame your content, rather than just posting catalogue-style images of your products and a "buy it now" link. Mums are much more likely to share a helpful article or video than they are a bland advert for your product.

9. Have a clear call-to-action

Mums have seen your message, now what? Social media serves to support broader business goals, so your messages should ultimately be tied to a larger purpose beyond being seen or liked. With that in mind, end your social posts with a strong call-to-action. This could include encouraging people to sign up for a free trial of your product, asking them to use a special social media code for an in-store discount, or giving them the opportunity to win some of your products in exchange for signing up to your newsletter.

10. Admit when you mess up

Part of being human is making mistakes, and with the fast nature of social media, mistakes are bound to happen. That's OK! Own up to it, apologise and move on. It'll make you more relatable.

When JoJo Maman Bebe boss Laura Tenison accidentally posted a highly critical message intended for the moderators to over 20,000 members of a Facebook group, she issued a quick and highly-relatable apology.[48] "Late-night posting is never a good idea," she said. "I had just come back from watching Trainspotting 2. I'm human and I made a mistake."

The apology was well-received by the group's members, most of whom could see the funny side, with many even going so far as to share their own examples of late-night faux pas.

Similarly, when McDonald's tweeted "Black Friday ****Need copy and link****" to their 3.5 million followers, rather than delete it, they followed it up with a second tweet that read: "When you tweet before your first cup of McCafé... Nothing comes before coffee." This simple acknowledgement of their mistake attracted more than 100,000 likes, making it the brand's most popular tweet of 2017.

What is all boils down to is being human. Ideally you want your posts to be crafted in such a way that they blend into users' new feeds and are relevant to their interests. Showing a human element and personality in your social media stream goes a long way towards achieving this aim.

Start and join conversations, offer insights and opinions, share useful content, and above all, be relatable. All of these aspects work together to create an active, engaged social audience—and will help build your brand trust, which is key when it comes to persuading mums to part with their cash.

There no hard and fast rules when it comes to promoting your brand through social media. Ultimately, it's about striking a balance between being authoritative and helpful versus being seen to be blowing one's own trumpet. Only by experimenting will you find out what resonates best with your target market.

Over to you

What are other businesses in your industry doing to drive engagement and raise their profile on social media? Are your competitors using a certain social media marketing channel or technique that seems to be working particularly well for them? If so, consider trying the same thing yourself, but do it better!

"

Alone we can
do so little.
Together we can
do so much.

"

- Helen Keller

8.

WHEN PR MEETS MARKETING: A LESSON IN INTEGRATION

Some things are just better together

Improvements in technology coupled with shifts in consumer mind-set have significantly changed the face of retail over the past few years. In the past, if a mum was searching for a present for a friend or family member, she would typically have headed to the shops to look for inspiration. Nowadays, she is much more likely to seek inspiration and information online, and only venture into a store when she already has an idea in mind of what she is looking for.

Mums have access to more brands than ever before, and are exposed to literally hundreds of advertisements and marketing messages every day.[49] As products and niches continue to proliferate, mums are increasingly looking for trusted sources that can help them navigate multiple options and choose those that best serve their needs. The strongest brands are wise to this, and make use of every communication channel at their disposal (both digital and non-digital) to raise awareness, inform people about the features and benefits of their products and services, build trust, and ultimately drive their target audience to make a purchase.

One of the most effective methods to connect with mums and gain their trust is through public relations, or PR as it is more frequently termed. PR essentially involves getting positive coverage for a company and its brands in the media. An example of this might include a feature in a newspaper or an interview on a radio show. It could also take the form of a mention in an article outlining the top 10 products in your industry, which is a particularly powerful way of letting mums know that yours is a brand worthy of their consideration. Or it might take the form of a quote in a general-interest piece written by a well-known journalist, which can be hugely influential in establishing your brand's credibility in the eyes of mums.

Whether they're looking for a new brand of moisturiser or a mortgage provider, the fact is that mums are much more likely to be influenced by information they read in a quality newspaper or discussed on a consumer affairs programme on TV than they are by the claims of a paid advertising campaign. And yet despite this, it is astonishing how many marketers fail to factor PR into their marketing strategy. All too often, marketing, social media and public relations are treated as separate entities, with little understanding of how they can work together to provide a more consistent message, expand a company's network of potential customers, and drive greater returns. This, in my mind, is a greatly missed opportunity, and shows a lack of understanding of how mums acquire information and make their purchasing decisions.

When two worlds collide

There's an old saying: "Advertising is what you pay for, publicity is what you pray for." While advertising is an important part of any marketing strategy, press coverage and media attention is infinitely more powerful when it comes to getting mums to trust, desire and buy into your brand. Having a well-respected journalist or influential blogger mention your brand brings credibility and cachet in a way that an advert in a glossy magazine never can.

Getting press coverage for you business just makes sense. Not only does it add credibility to your brand, but it is also cheap. A low investment can reap a large return, compared to advertising which is a considerable investment, and in many cases leads to greater reach.

That's not to say that paid advertising isn't an excellent marketing form, because it is. But it is when advertising is paired with public relations that the magic truly starts to happen.

Consider Hatchimals, the must-have hot ticket item of Christmas 2016, for example. For those not familiar with them, Hatchimals are mechanical plush toys that come trapped inside a large egg that begins to hatch once removed from its box. Once "born", the Hatchimal chick progresses through three stages of life: baby, toddler and child – singing its own rendition of 'Hatchy Birthday' as it reaches each new milestone.

What is interesting about Hatchimals' success is that prior to its launch in October 2016, few people had even heard of, let alone seen the toy. And yet within a matter of weeks, stores around the world had sold out of Hatchimals, with desperate parents spending as much as £250 to secure them through eBay – more than four times their recommended retail value. The reason for this? For the most part, it was down to a well thought out, integrated marketing and PR campaign designed to maximise hype and raise awareness.

Long before Hatchimals Day, as the October launch day came to be known, Spin Master – the toy's creator – began releasing teasers to the media. "When toys launch at the New York Toy Fair, typically everyone can learn about them and see them. But Hatchimals were under lock and key – almost literally," said Anne Yourt, who worked on the company's PR strategy. "There was only one photo that was seeded to a news outlet of the egg, but there was nothing revealed about what was inside." [50]

The next phase saw Spin Master partnering with YouTube influencers to create videos of children's excited faces as they finally got to see inside the box.[51] Meanwhile, retailers were told to leave space for the Hatchimals on their shelves, with signs saying, "See what's hatching October 7th." This led to a prelaunch wave of media reports and influencer posts on social media, speculating about what might be inside the eggs.

CNN were the first media outlet to reveal the contents of the egg on October 7th, swiftly followed by Good Housekeeping, The Today Show, The View, The Tonight Show Starring Jimmy Fallon, The New York Times, The Wall Street Journal, BuzzFeed, Daily Mail and The Guardian, to name but a few. The level of interest that this media attention created was incredible, and within 24 hours of Hatchimals being unveiled to the public, many retailers reported having sold out of their entire season's stock – which, in turn, prompted more news coverage for the brand, raising the brand's profile even further.

The need for integration

While media attention was clearly a driving force behind Hatchimals' success, it is important to realise that it didn't live in isolation. As Tara Tucker, VP of Global Marketing Communications at Spin Master told Campaign Magazine, it was a fully integrated launch plan. "Every aspect, including TV, paid digital, sponsorship integrations, and retailer events, worked in concert with our earned media outreach and influencer engagement. They all played together in a strong integrated campaign."[52]

This integration was key. The campaign was successful because it utilised a range of different mediums, drip-feeding information to the public in a way that was designed to generate maximum buzz. The YouTube videos, the media coverage, the empty shelves in the stores, and of course, the paid adverts on TV all worked together seamlessly to make sure that Hatchimals were at the top of Santa's Wish List.

Advertising, PR, and social media are all effective ways to promote a company and its products or services, and most successful communications strategies will include them all. Advertising enables companies to push key messages, PR helps build credibility and create sustained and positive media exposure, while social media is great for engaging with customers and getting people talking about your brand. As the Hatchimals case study clearly demonstrates though, only when the three come together in one integrated campaign does the marketing machine work at full capacity.

Whether you outsource your PR and social media management or run them in-house, it is important that they don't work in isolation. Don't allow different divisions of your company to work in silos, and definitely don't wait until the point of launch to start thinking about your PR strategy. Understand, accept and appreciate the different – and complementary – impacts that each discipline can have on your business. Then use this information to develop realistic goals, expectations, and measures of success for your PR and advertising efforts.

Think about where your potential customers are in the purchasing process, and where you need them to be. Are most mums already aware of your product or service? If so, how much do they know about its benefits to them? And for those who do know such things, where do you sit in terms of order of preference in their consideration set? Are you in the preferred position, or do you sit in second place behind a rival brand?

If awareness is a big issue, you might want to focus your attention on advertising and promotional opportunities that put your brand in front of as many mums as possible, as quickly as possible. Conversely, if most of your customers are nearer the end of the purchasing process, a better strategy might be to look for opportunities that help establish your brand as an industry influencer, perhaps by using a more content-based approach.

This is a strategy that has worked particularly well for car seat brand Maxi Cosi. Together with rival brand Britax, the brand spearheaded a new campaign in July 2013 to introduce a new car seat sizing system in Europe called i-Size. Unlike existing legislation, i-Size is based on a child's stature rather than their weight. It does not replace existing fitting standards, but runs alongside them – the message being that car seats that conform to i-Size simply offer more protection.

To raise awareness of the campaign and educate parents of the benefits of buying an i-Size certified seat, Maxi Cosi launched a widespread PR campaign. Through this the company were able to reaffirm their position as market leader by ensuring that pretty much every article ever written on the new car seat regulations either mentioned Maxi Cosi car seats, or at the very least, featured a quote from one of the brand's top "safety experts".

The campaign couldn't have been better timed. Just as the idea of extended-rear-facing was starting to take root in the UK, with Scandinavian brands such as BeSafe starting to see their extended rear-facing seats being stocked by Mothercare and other mainstream retailers, Maxi Cosi successfully found a way to bring industry stalwarts such as themselves back into focus. From a marketing perspective, it was nothing short of genius.

Lighting the way to increased sales

Nice as it is to have people talking about your brand, you need to make sure that you are communicating with mums in a way that moves them towards a purchase. When thinking about how to craft your own communications campaign, keep these six M's in mind:

1. **Market:** Who are you addressing? Are you speaking to the right target and are you crafting messages that are specific to them? Keep in mind that your market may include not only the mums you hope to sell to, but also the retailers and suppliers responsible for distributing your products.

2. **Mission:** What is your objective? Don't let your messages stray from that end goal. If your campaign objective is to increase brand awareness, then messaging should be more along the lines of "Learn More" rather than "Apply Now."

3. **Message:** What are the specific points you want to communicate? Mums may primarily be interested in the features and benefits of the product, but potential stockists and retailers will likely be more interested in the terms of trade, the

speed of shipping, volume discounts, and your efforts to generate demand through advertising.

4. **Media:** What communication vehicles are you using to get your message across? One medium is seldom enough—but too many may pose a risk of sending mixed messages.

5. **Money:** How much money can you afford to spend on the campaign? How can you perfect your combination of mediums to maximise your budget?

6. **Measurement:** How will you assess the impact and effectiveness of your communication efforts? Having a solid plan in place for measuring results will help keep you focused and enable you to make key decisions about how best to allocate your funds in the future.

PR is clearly a powerful tool for reaching mums, but it is important to recognise that a single press release is unlikely to significantly change the fate of your company. Instead, you must learn to use it in conjunction with other communication channels and promotional strategies. Simply coordinating your marketing and communications efforts isn't enough, either. You must also make sure that each activity represents your product or brand in a consistent manner. You don't want to run a series of Facebook adverts promoting your new breakfast cereal as a healthy choice for kids when the box screams "sugar". Such inconsistencies confuse customers and undermine brands.

The best way to avoid inconsistency is to put yourself in the shoes of the mums you are trying to target. Do the messages you are sending them create a clear, consistent and attractive image of your product? Are the physical characteristics of the product consistent with the message being distributed through print and social media, and through your advertisements? Do they reinforce and complement one another?

Think of your communications strategy as a musical orchestra. All the instrument sections may perform perfectly, but unless they play in the same key and harmonise, they will always sound more like a cacophony than a symphony. However, get them working together as one, and the result will be an altogether more powerful flow of coordinated notes.

Over to you

Conduct a thorough audit of your communications channels, and think about how aligned your social media, PR and paid advertising campaigns are in terms of delivering a consistent and unified brand image to mums in your target market.

"

The best advertising
is done by satisfied
customers.

"

- Philip Kotler

9.

THE ART OF HUSTLE
(AND THE NEED TO THINK
STRATEGICALLY)

Opportunity is the lifeline to success

A couple of years ago, my very talented and highly creative mother started making knitted caricatures of famous people. She started with the Royal Family, and then ahead of the 2015 UK General Election, moved on to knitting politicians. Initially, she just put them on display in her front window. Then, spurred on by all the lovely comments she received from passers by, she decided to tweet photos of her creations to then Prime Minister David Cameron, and to opposition leaders Ed Milliband, Nick Clegg and Nigel Farage. But sadly, despite her best efforts, her tweets were met with silence.

It was at this stage that I suggested she try targeting one of the lesser-known party leaders. Since David Cameron, Ed Miliband and Nigel Farage had over half a million followers each, I figured the chances of them actually seeing a tweet they were tagged in was extremely slim. Natalie Bennett – leader of the Green Party – on the other hand, had just 60,000 followers, which made her far more accessible. My mum got out her knitting needles, and started work. A day later, and as a direct result of Ms Bennett retweeting a photo of herself in knitted form, Buzzfeed were on the phone, swiftly followed by the Mirror. By the end of the week, my mum had been featured in nearly all of the national newspapers, been interviewed on BBC Radio, appeared on the ITV evening news, and been the subject of literally thousands of tweets. Nigel Farage passed comment on his knitted effigy in the press. And a few days later, my mum was thrilled to find retail queen Mary Portas on her doorstep after hearing about the knitted dolls from a friend.[53]

I tell you this story not to brag about my family's accomplishments, but rather to highlight the need to think strategically when trying to get your products "out there". New business ventures take off because the founders make them take off. There may be a handful that have managed to grow by themselves, but usually it takes some sort of push to get them going.

Two entrepreneurs who understood this need to

hustle are Julie Pickens and Mindee Doney, founders of Boogie Wipes. Thanks to a combination of good product development, strong marketing, and tactical distribution, their company, which makes gentle saline nose wipes for babies and toddlers, managed to turn over more than $1 million in their first year.[54]

Like many entrepreneurs, the founders went to a lot of trade shows, and spent a lot of time handing out free samples, soliciting feedback, and researching as they went. But for Pickens and Doney, this was just the start. They left samples in doctors' offices and kids' clothing stores. And not just in their local neighbourhood, either. They sent boxes of wipes to paediatricians all over the country, asking them to help spread the word. By doing this, they were able to generate feedback and exposure simultaneously. This also gave them a sizeable customer-base that they could leverage when pitching to retailers, and ultimately helped them secure a large order from Kroger, one of the world's largest grocery retailers.[55]

Generating buzz through word-of-mouth

In both the examples above, much of their success can be attributed to their ability to get their products seen and talked about by the right people. Both had fantastic products, they just needed to spend some time identifying key people who might be able to help get more eyes on their products. This was less about identifying who the products would appeal to the most, and more about figuring out would be most likely to talk about and share information about the products with their wider networks of contacts, and help set them on a path towards wider discovery.

Word-of-mouth is, without a shadow of a doubt, the most powerful form of marketing there is, and the more people you can get talking about your brand, the better. Remember the Hatchimals toy that we discussed in Chapter 8? The insane amount of press coverage the brand received in the days following its launch ensured the toy was the talk of the school gates for weeks. Be it where to get one, whether they were worth the cost, or simply passing judgement on the vast numbers of people paying over the odds to get one on eBay, the fact is that mums everywhere were talking about the brand, boosting awareness and ultimately, turning it into one of the most sought-after products of the year.

Pokemon Go is another great example of a product that relied heavily on word-of-mouth. Despite the company behind the app, Niantic, doing very little in the way of paid promotion, Pokemon Go quickly became the most downloaded app of 2016, making a very cool $950 million for the app's creators.[56] How did they do this? Mostly by encouraging players to share screenshots and other user-generated content that ensured the title stayed on the lips of the masses, even if many of them hadn't even played it yet.

When push comes to nudge

Many of us are swayed by what our friends are doing. Accordingly, sometimes all it takes is a little nudge to get customers to act. Nudge marketing is exactly what it sounds like: compelling consumers to behave in a desired manner by "nudging" them with a marketing message that straddles the delicate balance between being too soft and subtle and being too heavy handed and forceful.

Supermarkets have been experimenting with this technique for years. In one experiment, for example, a supermarket placed a strip of yellow duct tape down the middle of their shopping trolleys and instructed customers to put fruit and vegetables in one half, and their regular shopping in the other half. This simple little trick resulted in customers buying, on average, more than twice the amount of fresh fruit and veg that they normally would.

In another experiment, signs were places throughout the produce section, informing customers of the average number of pieces of fruit and vegetables purchased per customer. This again led to increased sales, by playing off the fact that most people like to follow social norms.

Another example of nudge marketing is the way hotels around the world now place signs in their rooms asking guests to help them "save the environment" or "save the earth" by reusing their towels. The signs are written in such a simple and unobtrusive way that you actually start to feel guilty if you don't reuse your towels. Can you guess how effective it is? It's helped hotels to save on average 2,300 litres of water and 150 litres of detergent each month.

The Training and Development Agency for Schools is yet another example of an organisation that has successfully incorporated nudge marketing into their strategy. When their TV adverts encouraging people to think about teaching as a career failed to generate enough leads, they decided to change direction and focus instead on offering help and support with the application process, thereby pushing people beyond simply thinking about teaching as a career and actually getting them to start making an application. According to Mike Olson, head of marketing at the TDA, this resulted in a record year for teacher recruitment.[57]

When trying to come up with an effective nudge, it helps to work backwards. Think about your end goal, and then work out what you can say or do to encourage mums to reach that point. Of course, many of you reading this right now will likely say your goal is simply to increase sales. In this case, the most effective nudge might be simply to introduce a higher-priced "premium" product that boosts revenue by making your second most expensive item seem better value for money. This "decoy" technique is most commonly used in the restaurant industry, where profit margins are frequently highest on the second most-expensive item on the menu.

Power of referrals

As we have seen, when it comes to shopping for new products – especially for their children – mums value the opinion of others. Whether they are looking for a new car seat or a Christmas stocking filler, mums will spend a significant amount of time researching the product online and seeking feedback from others before deciding whether or not to purchase a particular product or brand.

Let's look at some facts. According to Nielsen, 92% of consumers believe recommendations from friends and family over all forms of advertising.[58] However, two-thirds (66%) also said that they trust reviews posted online, highlighting the fact that trust isn't confined only to those in our inner circle. Further, in a survey commissioned by the American Marketing Association, 64% of marketing executives indicated that they believe word-of-mouth to be the most effective form of marketing. And yet, only 6% claimed to have mastered it.[59]

The main challenge with word-of-mouth marketing is that it is notoriously difficult to engineer. Sometimes, word-of-mouth is triggered when a customer experiences something far beyond what was expected – such as the time a bereaved mother contacted Tesco to ask for their help sourcing a blanket similar to the one that she had wrapped her stillborn baby in weeks earlier, only to have two store representatives turn up the next day not just with the blanket, but also with a card and a big bouquet of flowers. When the mum in question posted the story on social media, it immediately went viral, receiving more than 1,000 shares and 22,000 likes in less than 12 hours.[60]

Other times, word-of-mouth results after a mum discovers a solution to a particular problem or struggle. If one mother announces to her friends that her baby has started sleeping through the night after using a swaddle suit, her friends will likely want one too, and later their friends, and then their friends, and so on.

So just how do you go about encouraging conversations that help boost your brand? Fortunately, there are a few things you can do to encourage word-of-mouth referrals:

- **Ask for them!**
  A lot of companies miss out on word-of-mouth referrals because they're afraid to ask their customers to recommend their services. Don't be. If you provide an excellent product or service and have customers who are happy with your work, ask them to recommend you on social media or write a product review on a customer review site.

You'll probably find your most enthusiastic customers already talk about you, but they may not have thought to write about you online.

- **Find influencers with a relevant fan-base**

  A recommendation from a customer is powerful. But a recommendation from someone influential who has hundreds of thousands of online followers can be even more beneficial. Look for bloggers or social media influencers who have strong links with the sorts of mums you are trying to target, and follow them for a few weeks to see if they might be a good fit for your brand. Then reach out to them to discuss possible partnerships and collaborations. Some will happily promote your products in exchange for a free product sample or service trial, while others will expect to be paid for their time.

- **Encourage online reviews**

  Although it isn't the same as a personal recommendation, online reviews can give a customer the nudge they need to give your business a try. Encourage mums to leave reviews by including links in your purchase confirmation emails and on your website, perhaps offering to include them in a prize draw as a way of thanking them for their time.

- **Surprise and delight**

  Little things can go a long way in encouraging mums to recommend you to others. That could be anything from providing top-quality service to settling a customer service complaint in an above-and-beyond manner. There are several things you can do to surprise and delight your customers, including offering freebies and sending personalised thank-you notes. Both provide photo opportunities that stand out on newsfeeds when your customers receive them. While there's no guarantee you'll get a referral from this type of behaviour, if you routinely go the extra mile for your customers, you'll find you get more word-of-mouth recommendations than if you didn't.

Think before you act

Ultimately, it all boils down to strategy. All too often, business owners think of marketing as tactics to dial up revenue, with little thought given to how best to employ these tactics – or indeed, whether it's best to deploy them at all. They run competitions on Facebook because they think that is the best way to get mums to notice their brand; they tweet influencers with the largest following they can find in the hope that they will fall in love with their product and re-tweet it to their millions of followers; they focus on building likes on social media rather than engagement, believing that size is what matters most.

Strategy involves looking at the bigger picture. It is knowing your goals and coming up with a plan to achieve them. Tactics, conversely, are the tools that will help you get there.

While solid tactical execution is important, strategy ensures the right activities are done well and in the right order to maximise return. As the Chinese philosopher and military man Sun Tzu once quipped, "Strategy without tactics is the slowest route to victory. Tactics without strategy is the noise before defeat."

Put the right strategy in place, and you'll find that your customers will do much of the work of your marketing department for you by enhancing word-of-mouth promotion. This is true no matter how large or small your business is, or in what industry it operates.

Strategy may not always be as fun as creating ads or Snapchat ideas. But marketing without it more often than not results in spending far too much time and money on activities that will have no direct impact on the future scalability of your business. It's the equivalent of a doctor starting surgery before knowing a patient's history, studying their test results, or making a diagnosis. Or in other words, firing shots before setting your sights on the target.

Over to you

Use the marketing canvas on page 125 to map out your strategy. Note, this is not designed to be an in-depth marketing plan, but rather a brainstorming activity that will help focus your thoughts.

1. **Product:** what are you selling?
2. **Key message:** What is the single most important thing you want to tell mums about your product?
3. **Target audience:** What do the mums you are trying to market to have in common? What defines them?
4. **Unique marketable elements:** What is special about your product and differentiates you from your competitors?
5. **Audience influencers:** Where do your targets mums seek inspiration? Who influences them?
6. **Free channels:** What free channels will you use to reach your target group of mums?
7. **Paid channels:** What paid channels will you use to reach your target group of mums?
8. **Goals:** What are your campaign goals? What are you hoping to achieve?
9. **Performance metrics:** How will you measure the success of your marketing activities? What metrics will you measure in order to stay on track?

MARKETING CANVAS

Product	Key message	Target audience

Unique marketable elements		Audience influencers

Free channels	Paid channels	Goals	Performance metrics

"

When you talk,
you are only repeating
what you already know.
But if you listen, you may
learn something new.

"

- Dalai Lama

10.

BRANDS THAT UNDERSTAND

Recognising success

When it comes to marketing their products, the brands that fare well with mums all have one thing in common: they **recognise** which mums they should be targeting, **research** their needs, **respond** with a suitable offering, and **resonate** with mums in their marketing communications. These four Rs, as we shall call them, are an essential part of every successful brand campaign.

1. **Recognise**

   Brands that appeal to mums recognise the influence that mums hold, and understand the pressures and pleasures in mums' lives. They recognise that not all mums are created equal, and

127

tailor their products and packaging accordingly. Their marketing messages reflect the fact that mums are people in their own right, defined by their skills, abilities and passions, and not just by the fact that they have children. They don't base their campaigns on outdated stereotypes, and understand that motherhood isn't the only thing that defines the women they are targeting.

2. **Research**

Brands that are successful at targeting mums spend time researching and getting to know their customers. They build and constantly update enormous market research databases that give them a longitudinal view of attitudes, category use, appetite for new products. They appreciate the importance of style and design, and don't just take a standard product and hope to win mums over by "making it pink," but instead, base their decisions on extensive interviews and focus groups conducted with members of their target market.

3. **Respond**

Brands that understand mums respond to insight gleaned through research with well-thought out products and services that genuinely make mums' lives easier. They understand that mums are

FIGURE 10-1: The 4Rs of success

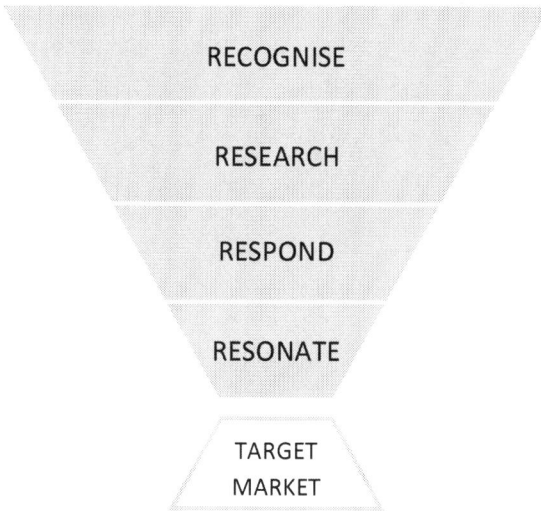

RECOGNISE

RESEARCH

RESPOND

RESONATE

TARGET
MARKET

looking for goods and services that leverage time, offer value for money, make their lives easier, deliver comfort, and are environmentally and socially responsible, and respond with simple, straightforward solutions that address the problem they have identified.

4. **Resonate**

Brands that resonate with mums don't patronise their target market, or assume that they are prudes. Nor do they depict motherhood as a series of mundane tasks to be completed or an experience that must be viewed through a lens of pastel perfection. Instead, they take time to get to know the woman behind the mum and come up with credible ways to engage.

Ultimately, the power of a brand lies in the minds of its customers, namely in how they experience the brand and their perception of it based on their past encounters and interactions with the brand. This is a crucial point. As has been said many times in the past, perception is reality. However well a company thinks it is doing at reaching out and delivering a benefit or value to mums, if the very mums they are targeting have a poor view of what is on offer, then the campaign will never take off. Companies that succeed know that when it comes to marketing, the only opinion that matters is that of their target customers.

In order for a brand to successfully target mums, they must perform well on the four Rs. Companies that do a good job of marketing to mums recognise the importance of mums in their category, do considerable research into the wants and needs of families, and respond with distinct offerings presented in a way that resonates with their target market. Above all, they listen to mums. They take time to understand mums' frustrations and identify opportunities for transformation.

P&G and the agents of change

According to research by the Institute of Mums, housework is one of the biggest sources of conflict in family homes, which is perhaps unsurprising given that mums typically spend three times as long on domestic chores as their husbands or partners.[61]

But while women are still largely responsible for the upkeep of the home, their routine has changed considerably in recent years, with time-pressed mums in particular now favouring spot cleans over deep cleans.

Global giant Procter & Gamble (the company behind such brands as Flash, Febreze, and Ambi-Pur) is undoubtedly one of the biggest beneficiaries of this change. But arguably, they are also one of the chief architects of the change too. The company's former CEO, AG Lafley (who retired in 2016 after 40 years at the firm) was a master at drawing insights from qualitative research and using them to come up with products that could be marketed as making mums' lives easier; products such as the Swiffer, a lightweight, easy-to-use sweeper fitted with a disposable wet or dry cloth that traps dirt and dust, rather than pushing it around as brooms and mops do, which generated more than $200 million of sales in the United States in its first year, and has since gone on to become one of Proctor & Gamble's top-selling products worldwide.[62]

Describing some of the factors behind P&G's success, Lafley said: "We're very much attuned to [a woman's] needs, her habits and practices, what she can afford, and what she really needs and what she really wants. I shop with mums when they are doing their weekly shopping, and get into their homes. I'm always in homes. I prefer to do the job with them so I can see what they are doing and what we can do better." [63]

Haier, the world's largest manufacturer of home appliances, is another good example of a company that conducts extensive research and then creates a product based on its findings.[64] Haier designs their refrigerators, for example, by considering women's height and the length or their reach, and configuring the compartments so that kids can serve themselves easily without having to ask mum for help.

Another company that has tailored its product based on feedback from mums is Premier Inn. The budget hotel chain commissioned research into what parents look for when looking for hotel accommodation, and found that parents want cheap and cheerful, spotlessly clean rooms, with separate beds for the kids (no wobbly camp beds) and generous floor space that allows plenty of margin for direct pathways to the bathroom in the night. Their research clearly paid off, with the users of Trip Advisor recently voting Premier Inn Britain's best family-friendly hotel chain.[65]

Family value

When deciding whether or not to buy a product or service, all consumers, and mums in particular, assess the value that they and their families will derive from its ownership. They consider its functional and emotional benefits, and compare it with similar products that they know or can find out about. They gather information about the product, read reviews and consider how a purchase will impact their lives and their relationships with others. They then put all these factors – often subconsciously – into an unspoken formula that enables them to determine a product's value to them at that particular time, and decide whether its price justifies its purchase. When the perceived value exceeds the asking price, they will bite, and when it doesn't, they will return it to the shelf and move on to something else.

Home furnishings retailer Ikea is particularly good at appealing to its customers' sense of value. Founded in 1943 by the Swedish entrepreneur Ingvar Kamprad, the brand is built on the back of simple cost-cutting strategies that enable the company to provide stylish yet functional products at lower costs, making them more accessible, without diminishing their quality.

Ikea appeals to women across demographic categories by offering its distinctive combination of quality and affordability. The retailer has a firm hold of the mummy market too, offering a range of brightly coloured yet highly practical products that appeal to both parent and child. One of their best-selling products, for example, is the Antilop high chair, which is easy to clean, comes apart for easy storage and is a bargain at just £14.

The store wins among parents in the fun stakes too. Most stores feature indoor and outdoor play areas, while the arrows on the floor guiding shoppers around the store and the numbered aisles in the self-service warehouse provide ample opportunities for parents to keep their children engaged while shopping. For many families, a trip to Ikea is quite literally seen as a fun day out.

Tesco is another retailer that understands the importance of keeping kids happy. In 2016, the supermarket operator began offering free fruit for children to munch on while their parents shop. The scheme was introduced after Maria Simpson, a Tesco checkout colleague from a store in Lincolnshire, suggested giving free fruit to parents for their children to eat during shopping trips as an alternative to sweets. The idea was taken up by the store and was so well received by customers that Tesco decided to roll out the initiative across all its major stores.[66]

If we are to learn anything from these retailers, it is that when marketing to mums, we cannot ignore the influence that their children have on their purchasing habits. Mums may hold the purse strings, but their children – if not the primary users of the products being purchased – are often heavily involved in the buying process in one way or another. Accordingly, as many retailers have found, even something as simple as having a small table in the corner laid out with colouring sheets can make the difference between a mum spending 2 and 20 minutes in the store.

Dove and the importance of keeping it real

Another way brands are seeking favour with mums is by backing issues and causes that people feel passionate about. Whether it's phone companies encouraging children to become interested in science, or supermarkets only stocking Fairtrade products, many brands are finding that backing good causes can be good for business.

One of the pioneers and indeed most sophisticated adopters of this so-called cause-based approach to marketing is Dove. For over a decade, the beauty brand has championed natural beauty through its campaign for real beauty, rejecting the traditional, superficial kind of fashion-industry images of stick-thin models with perfect hair and perfect skin in their adverts, in favour of normal-looking women of varying sizes and skin-colours. The campaign appeals to women everywhere, especially mums, tapping into their concerns about negative pressure from the fashion industry and the influence that it is having on their children.

In another campaign designed to get people talking

about their new Baby Dove line, the brand challenged the 'perfect mum' stereotype by reminding parents that there is no such thing as the perfect parent, only 'real' ones. The campaign video featured seven different mums who all face different challenges that affect the way they raise their kids. There's a mum raising her son on a cattle ranch, a mum who takes her baby on rock climbs, a transsexual mum and her wife who constantly have to explain that they are both their child's mother, a mum who refuses to give up her career as a dancer, a single mum, and a mum who's just learning what it even means to be a mum. All of these women have incredible stories, and all of their stories are different. The point is that even though each of these seven mums is raising their kids differently, they're all good mums. It seems obvious, but it's an effective message that resonates strongly with mums, nine out of ten of whom feel pressure to be a 'perfect parent' according to Dove's pre-campaign research.[67]

Alison Fisher, marketing manager for Unilever, admits initiatives such as these are about brand awareness, affinity and equity, as it associates Dove with "doing good". But there are also wider reasons for its continued focus on changing people's body image. "We genuinely want to make a difference here and lead by example. We have been running our own Dove Self-esteem Project for almost 13 years. We do really walk the talk in terms of what we do. It's about impact as well," she said in an interview with Marketing Week.[68]

Dads change nappies too

As any marketer will tell you, once you've managed to connect with your customers on an emotional level, you're far more likely to persuade them to part with their cash. If you can engage mums about their deepest concerns, respond with a relevant product and launch it with authority and conviction, then you will be well on the way towards capturing market share.

One brand that knows how to create and maintain a lasting emotional bond with mums is Pampers. Take, for example, the nappy brand's most recent ad campaign, which was filmed inside the Neonatal Unit at Southampton General Hospital. The moving footage – which is accompanied with a beautiful song titled 'I'm Coming Home,' documents premature babies through their first smile, first cuddle and, for some, their first journey home.[69] The advert generated an outpouring of emotional responses from mums across the UK, quickly finding its way onto Facebook and other social media platforms, where entire communities of mums came together to watch, rewatch and comment on the joys and terrors of motherhood.

Resonant as the ads are, however, they are not the main reason why Pampers has managed to maintain its position as the UK's best-selling nappy brand. The primary factor behind the brand's success lies in their consistent practice of listening to mums and delivering products that satisfy their needs. With a panel of 2,000 parents who test products weekly and give their opinions, Pampers is able to stay on top of what its target market needs, and refine their products as necessary.

One area where Pampers have recently made several changes lies in their relationship with fathers. The brand conducted a survey of parents in which 69 percent of men responded that they changed nappies as often their wives, while 11 percent said they did so even more often. Although men's perceptions differ from women's (only 31 percent of mothers said fathers split nappy duties equally, and just 4 percent said fathers did more), the findings are consistent with other reports about men's growing involvement in the home.[70] As a result, the brand is now experimenting with ways to incorporate dads more into their marketing.

"The role of dads is expanding and we salute that and we want to make dads a bigger part of the brand," said Bryan McCleary, a Pampers spokesman,[71] adding that Pampers now have a designated section on their website aimed exclusively at dads and dads-to-be.

Certainly, in order for brands to fully connect with mums, it is important for them to recognise the contribution that dads make. Brands need to understand that dads can be just as involved in parenting as mums, and take care not to isolate fathers, but instead communicate to the 'parenting unit' – without alienating single parents in the process (single parent families account for around a quarter of households with dependent children in the UK, according to the ONS).[72]

Similarly, brands must recognise that mums and dads are turned off by the 'dad as doofus' stereotype that has been so prevalent in recent years. Indeed, with dads now heading up 14% of all single-parent households in the UK, brands must cast their nets wider and start to represent dads doing more than just playing the fool if they are to reach their full potential.[73]

"I don't tend to get upset when I see a product focus only on mums in a commercial," blogged one father in a post about the failure of advertisers to connect with dads. "I work in marketing, so I understand the idea behind targeting certain demographics. The problem is making sure you're aiming at the right targets, and not failing by omission. I'm not going to stop buying a product just because they only market to mums, but I'm naturally inclined to purchase one that includes all types of parents. Including smart, adept, involved dads can only help." [74]

One company that has got the balance spot on is VW. In one advert centred around the morning school run, we see embarrassed kids trying to sneak out of their cars as quickly as possible, barely acknowledging the poor parent who has driven them there.[75] However, the girl arriving with her Dad in a VW Tiguan is totally cool, turning up the rap music ("Hip Hop" by Dead Prez) via her phone and winding down the window to show off to her mesmerised classmates. The school arrival's been done before in car ads, but this one has a fun twist – when Dad gets a little carried away by trying to fist-bump his daughter, which is met with a look of disgust that any parent of teenage children knows only too well!

As humorous as the advert is, the main reason it works is because it shows mums and dads both taking part in the same uneventful activity. That is, it reflects an ordinary scenario that both parents can easily identify with. And as Huffington Post blogger Zach Rosenberg recently wrote, "sometimes featuring fathers in a commercial is best when the father's presence *isn't* lauded or made overly-special." [76]

Celebrating imperfection

Whether they are a stay-at-home parent or a work-away-from-home parent, most parents find it much easier to relate to those who they perceive to share their weaknesses – those who mirror, or at least seem capable of mirroring the mistakes they tend to make.

The savviest brands are aware of this, producing some of the most memorable and relatable campaigns as of late – ads such as the Volkswagen advert described above, or the Kraft one described in Chapter 3, for example.

Ask parents how they approach parenting, and most will tell you they're just "winging it". Perfect home, perfect kids, perfect life; parents are tired of the flawless and faultless mother archetype (and the largely absent or clueless dad) that media and advertising continue to exalt. What they would much rather see are ads that reflect parenting as it really is: full of love, laughter and learning, and sometimes, just really darn tough!

Ultimately, it comes down to authenticity. Babies make a mess when they eat, and older children come out of school tired and grumpy. Ads that reflect this will always resonate more with parents than those pushing perfection. Instead of offering up idealistic personas that mums struggle to relate to, show them a little imperfection. Embrace the human experience, and let parents know that your brand understands them.

Over to you

Imagine you have been asked to write a report card for your competitors. Using the 4R framework, rate your competitors' brands based on your own perceptions, both as a competitor and as a consumer. Now try to evaluate your own brand. Try to look at it through the eyes of your target customers rather than from your own insider's perspective.

" However beautiful the strategy, you should occasionally look at the results. **"**

- Winston Churchill

11.

THE KEY TO LONG-TERM SUCCESS

Entice, delight, and grow

The true measure of success for a company is whether it stands the test of time. Sadly, not all businesses experience the longevity they crave. For every Facebook, there will be a MySpace; for every Instagram, a Flickr. The brands that survive are those that manage to consistently cut through the clutter and keep their brands current.

As we have seen time and time again, success begins with a solid understanding of customers. It is not simply a case of shouting your message louder than your rivals. Rather, the secret to success lies in packaging your message with something that mums value, and then coming up with a way to make sure that your brand remains at the forefront of customers' minds.

This largely explains why brands push so much money into sponsorship: by partnering with another global brand, they increase their exposure to a wider audience, and keep their brands at the forefront of people's minds. Nobody expects mums to rush out and buy a Volvo purely because the brand sponsors Game of Thrones and other popular TV programmes on Sky Atlantic, and yet the car manufacturer paid over £5 million for the privilege. The advantage for Volvo is that when a potential customer shops for a new car, the Sky Atlantic deal increases the likelihood they will think about the brand and therefore consider purchasing one of its vehicles.[77]

Similarly, brands like Dolmio, BT, Nivea and Boots don't sponsor ITV's This Morning programme because they need to increase brand awareness, but rather because they want to keep their brands top of mind among their target market. Like Volvo, these brands know that when it comes to marketing, one of the strongest markers of success is simply the customers' ability to recall their brand when considering a purchase.

Path to purchase: understanding how mums shop

Traditionally, it was thought that consumers followed a linear journey to brand purchase. The naïve customer first became aware of a brand, fell in love with some of its attributes, and consciously decided to purchase it. After personally experiencing the benefits for themselves they would hopefully become loyal advocates of the brand. Market research measured the proportion of consumers who had achieved each of these progressive steps and presented the facts to marketers in the shape of a neatly organised funnel.

Nowadays, it is generally accepted that the path to purchase is a little more complicated than this. The stages of awareness, consideration, decision and post-purchase evaluation still apply, but the journey itself has become more fluid. Instead of a path to purchase that is traditionally linear, it has become more of a cycle or even a web. Consumers move through and back and forth between the stages, influenced by a myriad of both offline and online factors at every stage.

Imagine that a mum decides to purchase a new pushchair. As with most kinds of products, she will immediately be able to name an initial consideration set of brands from which to choose. She will then begin reading up on these brands, seeking out online reviews, and speaking to others about their experiences and opinions on which pushchair might best fit her needs. Under the funnel analogy, we would typically expect the number of brands under consideration to reduce at this stage, as one-by-one, brands get dismissed, until just one clear winner remains.

The reality, of course, isn't nearly so straightforward. In fact, once mums start to research their intended purchase in more detail, it is not uncommon for the brands under consideration to change. Newer brands that weren't previously in the running "interrupt" the decision-making process, while others get displaced.

FIGURE 11-1: The four phases of the customer buying journey

BRAND AWARENESS

POST-PURCHASE EVALUATION

RESEARCH & CONSIDERATION

DECSION & PURCHASE

Eventually, of course, a decision will be made. But our job as marketers doesn't end here. In fact, when it comes to brand longevity, the post-purchase experience matters just as much as brand awareness. Positive customer experiences have always been critical in generating loyalty and repeat purchases. But as we discussed in Chapter 9, they also have the power to significantly influence other people's future buying decisions – both positively and negatively. For this reason, it is imperative that you keep track of what existing customers are saying about your brand, and continue to iterate and improve upon your marketing strategies as your brand grows.

The hidden cost of customer dissatisfaction

"We don't receive many complaints." This is something I often hear people say, as if it provides unequivocal evidence that they are delighting every customer who comes into contact with their brand. Unfortunately, however, it is not that simple.

According to research published by Technical Assistance Research Programs (TARP), when faced with disappointing service, only about 4% of customers complain to the company in question. The other 96% instead complain to their family and friends, or worse, post about it on social media, creating a possible exponential growth in the number of prospects who hear bad things about your company. Further, while satisfied customers tell eight people about their experience on average, dissatisfied customers will typically tell around 10 to 15 people.[78]

The mathematics of this is terrifying. For every complaint you receive, you could have as many as 24 disappointed customers that you know nothing about. What's more, collectively, these 25 customers could be telling more than 250 people about their bad experience with your company.

In order to have long-term success, customer experience must be at the forefront of all your marketing and branding endeavours. No longer can customer experience be an afterthought. It has to be at the epicentre of your brand's DNA. Whether you are looking for a competitive advantage, lower rates of customer attrition, or an increase in loyalty or revenue, focusing on the customer experience will pave the road to achieving those goals.

Measuring customer satisfaction through the Net Promoter Score

One of the most effective and highly regarded measures of customer satisfaction is the Net Promoter Score (NPS). This is a deceptively simple surveying technique that relies on the question "How likely is it you would recommend us to a friend?". Respondents are asked to return a numerical answer from 0-10, with ten being "extremely likely", and 0 being "extremely unlikely".

The scale is typically broken down as follows:

- Promoters (9 to 10): Customers who are not only satisfied, but enthusiastic, about your product. Most likely, they will continue to purchase and recommend the product to others.

- Passives (7 to 8): Customers who are satisfied with the product, but not necessarily excited about it. They may or may not recommend the product to others.

- Detractors (0 to 6): Customers who are dissatisfied with your product or with their experience with your organization. Detractors are unlikely to continue purchasing, much less recommend the product to others.

FIGURE 11-2: Net Promoter Score

"HOW LIKELY IS IT YOU WOULD RECOMMEND US TO A FRIEND?"

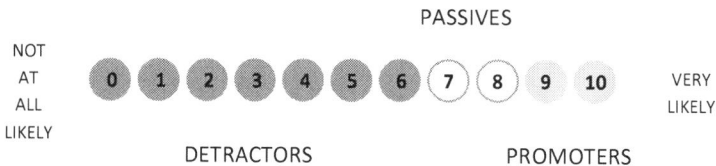

PASSIVES

NOT
AT
ALL
LIKELY

(0)(1)(2)(3)(4)(5)(6)(7)(8)(9)(10)

VERY
LIKELY

DETRACTORS   PROMOTERS

NPS = % PROMOTERS - % DETRACTORS

The Net Promoter Score is calculated by subtracting the percentage of detractors from the percentage of promoters, yielding a score between -100 to 100. A score of -100 means none of the respondents would recommend your brand to others, while a score of 100 means everyone is a promoter. NPS is an indicator of your company's health and is the first step to improving your customer's loyalty.

Some may scoff at such a seemingly simple metric, given the abundance of overly-complex metrics and customer data in existence today, but NPS should not be taken lightly. Widely used by Fortune 500 companies, it provides brands managers with quantifiable, usable feedback that helps them track customer sentiment over time. Further, research shows that the Net Promoter Score is THE leading indicator of growth. The higher an organisation's NPS, the higher the likelihood of outperforming competitors.

Staying true to your word

Marketers make promises: "Lowest prices", "Great taste", "Fast results", "Stain-free formula", "Good night's sleep, guaranteed." One of the primary challenges for companies is making sure that they deliver on these promises. The last thing we as marketers want to do is leave our customers feeling disappointed by our products or services, or feeling as though they received poor value for money.

While you're ploughing money into marketing and promotions to bring in new customers, it is essential that you don't forget about your existing ones. Your competitors are likely spending large amounts of money trying to come up with ways to make your customers their own. You, therefore, need to be speaking to your customers to find out what they think about your brand, what they would like done differently, and offering them promotions and loyalty bonuses that will hopefully keep them coming back for more. Your customers chose your brand for a reason, but don't let that be an excuse for stagnation. Even large companies with loyal customer bases are vulnerable to disruption.

Businesses that fare well with mums and manage to successfully hold their loyalty are constantly evaluating and improving their offerings while maintaining a consistent and recognisable brand experience. They prioritise customer experience above everything else, and regularly monitor how they stack up against their competitors.

You will never manage to please all your customers all the time, and that is ok. The best you can do is listen to their concerns or complaints, do what you can to diffuse the situation as quickly as possible, learn from your mistakes, and move on. Fighting too hard to keep a disgruntled customer is bad business. Remember, it is always better to give up on a sale or offer a refund than it is to make an enemy of a customer. Deal with complaints calmly and efficiently, and you'd be surprised how much goodwill it creates – in some instances even resulting in more brand loyalty than if the fault had not occurred in the first place.

It's the little things that count

When it comes to business, there are two main approaches, says Rory Sutherland, Vice Chairman of Ogilvy and Mather group.[79] There is the "tourist restaurant" approach, where you try to make as much money from people on their single visit. And then there is the local pub approach, where you may make less money from people on each visit, but where you profit more over time by making your customers feel valued enough to want to come back.

The coffee shop that provides mums with a second complimentary biscuit for their child is a good example of the second approach. It's a small gesture, but is a reliable signifier that you are investing in a repeat relationship, not milking a single transaction.

Similarly, the hotel that provides complimentary slippers in both child and adult sizes in their family rooms sends a nice message to parents that the hotel values their younger visitors as much as their business clientele. That Tesco provides free fruit for shoppers to give their children while shopping in-store is another example of a brand willing to go the extra mile for their customers.

Occasionally, a customer will give you the opportunity to provide them with a really memorable service themselves, such as in this next example. The story begins when customer Chris Hurn's son left his favourite stuffed giraffe, "Joshie," in their hotel room after a recent stay. Mr Hurn assured his distraught son that Joshie was just staying a few extra days on vacation, and called the hotel to see if they could return the toy. In an all-star effort to make everything right for the family, the staff at the hotel responded by not only sending the beloved toy home, but by creating a photobook showing all of the activities Joshie had been involved in during his "extended vacation."[80]

Value-based satisfaction

Every company says that their customers are their number one priority, but as the old cliché goes, actions speak louder than words. All too often, companies lose sight of their brand values as they focus on the day-to-day activities of their business. It happens more often than you think, and it happens because of the false belief that marketing is simply about creating a slogan and a logo that millions of people will recognise and remember.

It may not seem sexy, but the most effective way to achieve long-term success is to consistently deliver. These days, competition for customers is fierce. And while anyone can achieve short term gains through clever branding and positioning, ultimately, it is staying true to your values and delivering a consistent, desired experience that will earn your customers' trust and loyalty.

To successfully market to mums, you must make them feel like you care about them. Mums want to feel as though you have their families' best interests at heart and that you are trying to help them succeed in their parental role. By finding ways to delight your customers at every given opportunity and delivering them with a brand experience that is extraordinary not ordinary, you are sending them the message that you truly value and appreciate their business. Do this, and you are guaranteed a spot on the list of companies that knows how to successfully market to mums.

Over to You

Listening to your customers (and demonstrating respect) is a really underestimated value that a lot of businesses neglect. Take the time to sit down and think about what you are doing to delight your customers, and think about ways in which you can improve your service. If you aren't already, start tracking your customers' net promoter ratings as a way to monitor and track customer satisfaction over time.

CLOSING REMARKS

Marketing is as much about strategy as it is tactics. Many people think of marketing as being mostly concerned with the latter – sales, promotion, advertising, public relations, social media, and so forth, and indeed, this is where most marketing budgets seem to get spent. However, as the examples in the preceding pages have hopefully demonstrated, strategy, above everything else, is what differentiates great marketers from mediocre ones, and ultimately, is what enables a company to keep growing.

The question business owners need to ask themselves is not "What else can we do?" but rather "What else can we do for our customers?" It's no longer enough to have a superior product. In order to achieve maximum success, you must look at the needs of the mums you aim to serve and position your brand and products relative to their purchase criteria.

Today's market leaders are those that are able to clearly define what performance means in their respective categories: Maxi Cosi sets the bar on car seat safety, shaping parents' expectations for features from Isofix to side-impact protection systems; Febreze has changed the way customers perceive a clean house; Premier Inn has changed our perception of budget hotels; and Kraft and Heinz have revolutionised the way families eat.

A key part of a marketer's job is to influence how customers perceive the relative importance of various product attributes and sell them on the merits of your product offering as the best possible solution for their needs. How you position your product offering in the mind of mums, how you place yourself vis-à-vis your competitors within the marketplace, and of course your pricing, will ultimately determine how successful you are in achieving this.

Having completed this book, I would hope that you now feel empowered and inspired to create your own strategic marketing plans, and work out which tactics might serve you best. I hope that you have also come to understand and appreciate the need to conduct external market research with your target audience before embarking on any new marketing campaign. As much as I can advise you on marketing strategy and how best to achieve your marketing goals, only by taking time to listen to the mums you hope to serve and acting on their feedback, can you stay relevant and uncover the most efficient way to market your products and services.

Marketing your brand to mums needn't be expensive, but it does require some out-of-the-box thinking. It can also mean subjecting yourself to risk. But for those who are creative and brave enough to try, the rewards can be priceless.

Hungry for more?

The Institute of Mums® Academy offers a
series of digital courses, webinars
and bonus content for you to
access at your leisure.

Enter code: M2M

www.academy.instituteofmums.com

NOTES

1. Kind und Jugend is the world's largest trade show for baby and children's products, and is held every year in Cologne. For more info on this and other trade shows, see www.b-p-a.org/bpa-org/tradeshows.asp.

2. The statistic that 80 percent of companies fail within the first 18 months is widely quoted and referenced by respected news sources such as Bloomberg and Forbes. See www . bloomberg . com / news / articles / 2002 – 03 – / the – bottom–line–on–start–up–failures (subscription required) and www.Forbes.com / sites / ericwagner / 12013 / 09 / 12 / five-reasons-8-out-of-10-businesses-fail / #671742916978, for example.

3. The BPA Concept & Innovation Awards are open to both companies and individuals with innovative ideas for new maternity, baby, nursery and antenatal products. For more information, visit www.thebpa.eu.

4. A full list of previous winners can be found on the Harrogate Nursery Fair website: www.nurseryfair.com / bpa candi.asp.

5. After evaluating the 5 Point Plus Anti-Escape System, Maxi Cosi confirmed on 4th April 2014 that they would recommend the safety accessory to parents that contact them to ask for a solution for a child that is freeing himself from their harness. Maxi Cosi also promised to integrate the 5-point plus accessory in the FAQ section on their website. Further information detailing Maxi Cosi's endorsement can be found on the 5 Point Plus website: 5pointplus.com / recommended–by–maxi–cosi–and–bebe–confort.

6. Since 2014, CB Insights has parsed over 200 post-mortem

essays by startup founders and investors. According to their analysis, 42% of startups blame a lack of market need for their demise. A compilation of the startups' post-mortems, as well as further information on CB Insight's methodology can be found on their website: www.cbinsights.com/blog/startup–failure–post–mortem.

7. The phrase "Humility of Marketing" was first coined by Marketing Week columnist and Melbourne Business School professor, Mark Ritson. He defines it as, "The realisation that no matter how smart you might think you are as a marketer your main role is charting the stupidity of your customer and accepting that their perception must become your reality – whatever your own supposedly superior viewpoint on the issue."

8. In a rare 1990 video interview with Steve Jobs for PBS, interviewer Timothy Leary asked Jobs about the importance of market research and how much he relied on it. Jobs responded as follows: "Well you know I think in the early days it was very easy because you would go to a home group computer club meeting and there was your whole market and so you could find out what they thought. Now if you show them your product and see what they thought and you could because products were much simpler then and within a few months you could change it all around and come back and show the new one. But as the market got more sophisticated it was less easy to do that. And the problem is that market research can tell you tell you what your customers think of something you show them. Or it can tell you what your customers want as an incremental improvement on what you have, but very rarely can your customers predict something that they don't even quite know they want yet. So there are these sort of non-incremental jumps that need to take place where it's very difficult for market research to really contribute much in the early phases of thinking about how to you know what those

should be. However, once you have made that jump possibly before the products on the market or even after is a great time to go check your instincts with the marketplace and verify that you're on the right track." Source: www.youtube.com/watch?v=2U3w5Blv0Lg.

9. Ford produced their first car, the Model A, in 1903, but it wasn't until 1908 that the iconic Model T, Ford's masterpiece, was released. In the five years that spanned between the A and the T, Ford send mechanics out to collect feedback from customers; feedback that Ford immediately implemented in his assembly line. Speaking about the development of the Model T, Ford wrote in his autobiography: "Every detail had to be fully tested in practice. There was no guessing as to whether or not it would be successful." Source: Ford, H. My Life and Work. New York, 1922, p.70.

10. Tinder is a location-based social search mobile app that facilitates communication between mutually interested users, allowing matched users to chat. Although the app is most commonly used as for dating purposes, Tinder is working on a new iteration, Tinder Social, for groups of friends who want to hang out with other groups on a night out, rather than dating.

11. The Office for National Statistics (ONS) is the UK's largest independent producer of official statistics and is the recognised national statistical institute for the UK. It is responsible for collecting and publishing statistics related to the economy, population and society at national, regional and local levels. It also conducts the census in England and Wales every ten years. The ONS website can be found at www.ons.gov.uk.

12. To access statistics on spending patterns of UK households, see the Family Income and Expenditure Survey: www.ons.

gov.uk/peoplepopulationandcommunity/personalandhouse
holdfinances/expenditure.

13. The Freedom of Information Act 2000 provides public access to information held by public authorities. Requests must be made in writing. For information on how submit a request for statistical information from the ONS, see www.ons.gov.uk/aboutus/transparencyandgovernance/free domofinformationfoi/makingarequest.

14. To view the full range of electronic materials that can be accessed at the British Library, visit: http://electronic resources.bl.uk/sfxlcl41/az/londb.

15. Tinker Tailor Soldier Spy is a 1974 spy novel by British author John le Carré. It follows the endeavours of taciturn, aging spymaster George Smiley to uncover a Soviet mole in the British Secret Intelligence Service. Since the time of its publication, the novel has received critical acclaim for its complex social commentary, and remains a staple of the spy fiction genre.

16. The adage about there being a gap between what people say and what they do is a simplification of extensive writing by Margaret Mead on the fieldwork of anthropologists.

17. Shortly after being elected CEO of P&G, A.G. Lafley created a "consumer closeness programme" entitled Living It. This programme required P&G managers to spend time in the customers' environments to learn from their perspectives. A follow-up programme called Working It expanded upon the Living It model by having P&G staff function as sales counter clerks in various retail outlets. This enabled P&G personnel to develop insight into their customers' decision-making processes, and learn more about price point limitations, behavioural considerations, and alternative competitive product choices. To reinforce

these changes, Lafley led by example and went once a month to meet with P&G's customers. He indicated that this initiative "gave clarity and meaning to our business strategy… it pulled us together… it was crystal clear, compelling and inclusive." Source: Lafley, A.G. and Charan, R. The Game Changer. New York: Crown Business, 2008.

18. In the 1990s, 2.4 was the average number of children per household in the United Kingdom (also known as the total fertility rate). Although the average number of children has since fallen to 1.8, the phrase continues to be used when referring to stereotypical characteristics of normal family life.

19. There are 2 million maternal breadwinners in Britain, making up one third (33%) of mothers in working families, according to the Institute for Public Policy Research. The proportion of maternal breadwinners rose from 23% in 1996 to 33% in 2013. This growth predominately took place before 2011, at which point the rate stagnated. In Britain it was the increase in mothers in couple households becoming breadwinners that fuelled a substantial rise between 2008 and 2011. Although maternal breadwinning is more prevalent in low and middle-income households, the largest increases have been in the middle of the distribution. 37% of mothers in working families in the bottom half of the distribution are breadwinners, compared to 29% in the top half. This is due to female-led single parent families being more likely to be middle income earners, compared to couple households who are likely to be spread across income distributions. Source: www.ippr.org/ publications/ whos-breadwinning-in-europe.

20. Of the 2.9 million lone parent families in the UK in 2016, the majority (86%) were headed by a female lone parent, according to the ONS. Source: www. ons. gov. uk / people populationandcommunity/birthsdeathsandmarriages.

21. The number of foreign-born mothers having babies in England and Wales in 2016 reached 28% - the highest level on record. Poland the most common country of origin for foreign-born mothers, followed by Pakistan, and then India. Despite an overall decline in the number of live births in England and Wales between 2015 and 2016, births to women born outside the UK increased by 2.1%, due to foreign-born women making up an increasing share of the female population of childbearing age. Source: www.ons. gov.uk/ people population and community / births deaths and marriages / livebirths / bulletins / parents country of birth englandandwales/2016.

22. Although the percentage of births outside marriage continues to rise, it should be noted that the majority of these babies have parents who live together - over the last decade over 60% of all births registered outside marriage or civil partnership each year have been to a cohabiting couple. This is consistent with increases in the number of couples cohabiting rather than entering into marriage or civil partnership. For further information, see www.ons.gov.uk/ peoplepopulationandcommunity/birthsdeathsandmarriages /livebirths/bulletins/birthsummarytablesenglandandwales/ 2016.

23. The full advert is available to watch online at www.youtube. com/watch?v=U5NxumE2DVI.

24. Source: www.businesswire.com/news/home/2017050300 5471/en/Kraft-Mac-Cheese-Swears-Imperfect-Parenting-Perfectly.

25. For information on Dairylea's market share, see www.the grocer. co. uk / focus – on – lunchbox – health – sends – kids – chomping–cheese/211317.article (subscription required).

26. Source: Nielsen, Value Sales, Total Coverage, MAT data to

25.03.17 –via www.fdin.org.uk / 2017 / 05 / dairylea-takes-flavour-innovation-up-a-nach.

27. Brand equity is defined as a brand's power derived from the goodwill and name recognition that it has earned over time, which translates into higher sales volume and higher profit margins against competing brands.

28. This case study was first presented in Koselka, R. 1994. "Hope and Fear as Marketing Tools." Forbes 154 (5) Aug 29:78-79.

29. Ibid.

30. Field of Dreams is a 1989 American fantasy-drama sports film based on W. P. Kinsella's novel Shoeless Joe, and directed by Phil Alden Robinson.

31. The complete product model is a variation of the whole model framework suggested by Theodore Levitt in a 1980 Harvard Business Review publication.

32. Quoted in Sutherland, R. Wiki Man. London, 2011 (p.33).

33. Source: Christmas Survey of 1,218 parents by IOM Research, December 2016.

34. Ibid.

35. Source: Amazon Trends Report, 2016.

36. For additional commentary on the success of Fever-Tree, see www.ft.com / content / fd6d2f70 - 0e30 - 11e7 - a88c - 50ba212dce4d (subscription required).

37. Led by CEO Michael O'Leary, Ryanair is well-known for publicity stunts that are typically designed to shock and

entice the nations' press into inadvertently promoting the Ryanair brand. For examples of some of their more outlandish stunts, see: www.umpf.co.uk/blog/pr/ryanair-the-slag-of-the-cheap-pr-stunt.

38. When a 2-year-old boy with Autism grew out of his favourite pair of shoes, his mum tried to order a replacement pair from Mothercare, only to be told that they had been discontinued. She contacted Mothercare's Head Office, who responded by sending her a box full of the shoes, in various different sizes. When the boy's mum posted the story on Facebook, it quickly went viral, attracting over 36,000 shares, over 97,000 likes and over 10,000 comments.

39. In 2010, Graco announced a recall of 1.5 million strollers worldwide after 7 injuries were reported. The company set up a dedicated Web Page to deal with the recall, posted information on all their social media platforms, and reached out to top influencers to help share information, before sending out a press release. This gave them time to get ahead of the news and prepare their customer service teams. Their swift response in dealing with customer concerns was appreciated by customers, and even led to the Christian Science Monitor publishing an article praising the brand after seeing positive interactions between Graco and consumers on Twitter.

40. After staff at several branches of her favourite coffee shop refused to give her hot water to warm up her baby's milk, a mum from Swindon decided to post about her experience online. Her story was quickly picked up by a local newspaper, resulting in a significant amount of negative publicity for the popular high street coffee chain.

41. Although strange supermarket substitutions make for good stories, analysis by Which shows that online supermarkets

that don't make many substitutions, or stick to sensible ones, generally tend to rank higher in consumer surveys. Source: www.which.co.uk / news / 2017 / 03 / 13 – of – the – worst–supermarket–substitution–fails–revealed.

42. Case study quoted in www.nytimes.com / 2011 / 08 / 18 / business / Abercrombie–offers–jersey–shore–cast–a–paid–non–product–placement.html.

43. Source: www.salon.com/2006/01/24/jeffries.

44. Source: www.prweb.com / releases / 2014 / 09 / prweb12149 402. htm.

45. Interview excerpts taken from the Islabikes website: www.islabikes.co.uk / info–hub / designing–bikes – for – growing–bodies.

46. Interview excerpts from a talk delivered by Ian Watson to the Norfolk Network in July 2017. For a summary of the talk, see www.norfolknetwork.com / next–steps–new–ceo–ian–watson–takes–start–rite–shoes–modernising–journey.

47. A Facebook study based on 1.6 million new mums found that they spend 1.5X more time on Facebook than non-mums. By 7am, 56% of new parents on mobile have visited Facebook for their first mobile session of the day, compared to 45% of non-parents. Source: fbinsights. files. wordpress. com / 2015 / 09 / facebookiq _ moments _ whitepaper.pdf.

48. Source: www. thetimes. co. uk / article / baby – clothes – company–chief–attacks–online–second–hand–sales–33nf 70gp2.

49. Actual estimates vary depending on the methodology used. One 2005 study, for example, concluded that the number

could be as high as 3500 advertisements per day.

50. Spin Master's PR strategy was previously discussed in PR Week: www. prweek. com / article / 1419219 / hatchimals – became–years–toy–craze.

51. YouandMe and FUNnel Vision are two such influencers, their videos garnering over 20 million views combined.

52. Source: www. campaignlive. co. uk / article / 1419219 / hatchimals–became–years–toy–craze 1419286#QiAyBAoi ALgq7V6L.99

53. A selection of Pat Wilson's knitted caricatures can be seen at www.knittingimage.com.

54. Mindee Doney and Julie Pickens developed Boogie Wipes as a solution for their kids' sore, red, stuffy noses. Sales went on to reach $1 million in the company's first year of business and by 2009, their company, Little Busy Bodies, tripled its revenue to $3.4 million.

55. In June 2011, Little Busy Bodies expanded into the teen and adult market with the introduction of its second product line, Saline Soothers. The company now sells in 50,000 retail stores across the U.S. and Canada including Walmart, Target, Walgreens, and Toys 'R' Us.

56. Source: www.forbes.com/ sites/ryanwhitwam/2017/01/19 / Niantic–made–almost–1–billion–in–2016–so–why–is– pokemon–go–still–so–lame.

57. Via www. campaignlive. com / article / behavioural – econom ics–when–push–comes–nudge/1070184

58. Source: www. nielsen. com / content / dam / nielsenglobal / apac / docs / reports / 2015 / Nielsen – global – trust – in –

advertising–report–September–2015.pdf.

59. Source: American Marketing Association, Word of Mouth Advertising: Survey of Marketers, 2014.

60. For full story, see www . huffingtonpost . co . uk / entry / tesco–blanket–stillborn–baby_uk_5770ea52e4b08d2c56397 c16.

61. A survey of 1,800 households found that women spend an average of 17 hours a week on domestic chores, such as cooking, cleaning and washing, compared to just under 6 hours for their husbands or partners. Additional findings from the survey can be found here: www.dailymail.co.uk/ news/article-206381/Working-women-housework.html.

62. Swiffer is a line of cleaning products by Procter & Gamble. It is based on the "razor-and-blades" business model, whereby the consumer purchases the handle assembly at a low price, but must continue to purchase replacement refills and pads over the lifespan of the product.

63. Quoted in www.bloomberg.com/news/articles/2005–01–27/ lafley–on–p–and–gs–gadget–evolution.

64. Haier has been named the number one global home appliance brand every year for the last six years by Euromonitor International, a world leader in strategy research for consumer markets, and in 2012 the Boston Consulting Group named Haier one of the ten most innovative companies in the world as well as the most innovative company in the consumer and retail category. Its global headquarters is based in the Chinese city of Qingdao, with regional Headquarters in Paris and New York. Haier also has 5 R&D centres, 66 trading companies and 21 industrial parks worldwide. Source: www.prnewswire.com/ news – releases / haier – tops – euromonitors – major – app

liances–global–brand–rankings–for–seventh– consecutive–
year–300206919.html.

65. Source: www.premierinn.com/gb/en/news/2016/best-family-hotel.html.

66. For more on the introduction of the initiative, see www.tescoplc.com/news/news-releases/2016/free-fruit-for-kids-at-tesco.

67. Source: Baby Dove Real Mothers Heard study, 2016.

68. Quoted in www.marketingweek.com/2017/01/19/dove-body-confidence-authenticity.

69. Watch the advert online at www.youtube.com/watch?v=4eLEtCRRbxg.

70. Survey results via the New York Times. Source: www.nytimes.com/2010/06/23/business/media/23adco.html.

71. Quoted in: www.nytimes.com/2010/06/23/business/media/23adco.html.

72. Of the 2.9 million lone parent families in the UK in 2016, 14% were headed by a male lone parent. These percentages have changed little over the past 20 years. Source: www.ons.gov.uk/peoplepopulationandcommunity/birthsdeathsandmarriages/families/bulletins/familiesandhouseholds.

73. According to official statistics, men now make up nearly 10 per cent of those who care for children while their partner goes out to work. Via www.telegraph.co.uk/women/9822271/Rise–in–stay–at–home–fathers–fuelled–by–growing–numbers–of–female–breadwinners.html.

74. Quoted in: 8bitdad.com/2014/01/17/dad–bias–in–2013–

commercials–17917/3.

75. To watch the full commercial, see www. youtube.com/ watch?v=YLzC_b1Q5BE.

76. Quoted in: 8bitdad.com/2014/01/17/dad–bias–in–2013– commercials–17917.

77. As a direct result of the sponsorship, Volvo has seen significant uplifts in brand image scores for viewers who have seen the TV sponsorship ads. There were also uplifts in brand metrics such as likeability, consideration and recommendation.

78. Source: Tatikonda, L. The Hidden Costs of Customer Dissatisfaction. Management Accounting Quarterly; Spring 2013, Vol. 14 Issue 3, p.34.

79. Quoted in www . marketing society.com/the–gym/shadow –future#YJ8T6cy29TkFYrsi.99.

80. For the full story, see www.socialmediatoday.com/content / joshie – giraffe – remarkable – story – about – customer – delight.

ABOUT THE AUTHOR

Jessie Wilson is the founder and CEO of Institute of Mums, a specialist market research and insight agency. She has over 15 years' experience observing consumer trends and behaviour around the world through surveys, focus groups and other forms of research, and helping companies formulate and develop strategic marketing and brand plans. Some of the brands she has worked with include the BBC, Allianz, L'Oreal, Mamas and Papas, Disney and Dorel (the parent company of Maxi Cosi and Quinny).

Following a stint as Head of Baby Product Research at a London consultancy firm, Jessie set up Institute of Mums in 2015 to support clients within the family and baby-product industries. Part of this involved building a large social media presence that she can tap into and leverage for research purposes. The page has since become one of the UK's most popular parenting pages on social media, attracting as many as 3 million unique visitors every week.

Jessie has experience working across multiple industries, including luxury goods, leisure and tourism, fashion and beauty, consumer electronics, education, and nursery and toy products. She has authored more than 30 reports on various demographic and socio-economic issues, as well as numerous reports looking at various aspects of the nursery and toy industry. She was also a contributing author to Mr and Mrs Asia, which involved surveying more than 35,000 families across Asia.

Jessie is an accomplished presenter, and has spoken at numerous high-profile events and conferences. Her work has been featured in publications such as the Economist, the Financial Times, the Washington Post, the Times, the Daily Mail, and on the BBC, to name but a few.

She lives in Royal Tunbridge Wells, with her partner Philip and daughter Timi.

INDEX

Need quick, cost-effective market research?

Look no further!

Institute of Mums® is a full-service market research and insight firm, specialising in baby, child and family research. We offer both qualitative and quantitative services, ranging from market sizing and brand tracking to online focus groups, depth interviews and surveys of mums, dads, kids, grandparents, and other family members.

For a no-obligation quote, give us a call on 020-7193-7278 or visit www.iomresearch.com.

INSTITUTE OF MUMS® **IOM** Research

19393678R00114

Printed in Great Britain
by Amazon